SUZAN S

MW00817471

ASTROLOGY
FOR CHRISTIANS

Astonishing Evidence from History and the Bible

REDFeather™
MIND | BODY | SPIRIT

4880 Lower Valley Road, Atglen, PA 19310

**Dedicated to every person who was
led to mistrust astrology without
really knowing the reason why.**

Library of Congress Control Number: 2018957912

Designed by Danielle D. Farmer
Cover design by Brenda McCallum

Three wise men riding camel desert dusk © Rawpixel.com. Backdrop design of sacred symbols, signs, geometry and designs © whiteMocca. Courtesy of Shutterstock, Inc. Fragment of Astronomical Celestial Atlas: Stars Heavens Planets. © Green Ocean. Courtesy of Bigstock Images.
Type set in Cheltenhm BdCn BT/Minion Pro/Helvetica

ISBN: 978-0-7643-5722-0
Printed in the United States of America

Published by Red Feather Mind, Body, Spirit
An imprint of Schiffer Publishing, Ltd.
4880 Lower Valley Road
Atglen, PA 19310
Phone: (610) 593–1777; Fax: (610) 593–2002
E–mail: Info@schifferbooks.com
Web: www.redfeatherpub.com

CONTENTS

INTRODUCTION

Why is it so difficult for most contemporary people to consider the idea of astrology? From a very young age, we have been taught to reject astrology based upon a centuries-old misconception that originally found its way into early church doctrine and was carried down through the centuries. Whether we are religiously inclined or not, almost everyone born and raised within a typical American or western European environment does not stop to question, let alone explore, this basic misinformation. For most of us as adults, the early learning experience created a deep psychological bias against astrology. Clearly, this bias is based only upon what we have been told and not upon direct personal experience.

The purpose of this book is to provide indisputable evidence that the original misconceptions against astrology were deliberately initiated by authorities who were greatly sanctioned by the early Church of Rome, yet those authorities were unquestionably infused with severe political bias and were either not knowledgeable or frankly misunderstood the subject of astrology. Passed along through the ages, most of us have done little to question that authority. We reject astrology simply because other people and older generations have told us to do so.

This book will clarify and correct the disreputable reputation that has been inaccurately assigned to astrology. We will explore the ancient origins of astrology and provide an astounding amount of supporting and illuminating evidence found not only in history, but also within the Old and New Testaments of the Bible. In short, we will prove that, in fact, diametrically opposed to what we have been led to believe, astrology clearly and fundamentally follows the plan created by God.

It is now, within the cultural milieu of the modern Western world, that we should be asking ourselves the following question: If we found that astrology really does exist and is truly part of God's original creation, then what would happen next?

- We would need to change our entire way of looking at the world.
- We would find it necessary to believe more profoundly in the creative intelligence of God.
- Our cultural paradigm would dramatically shift.
- Our worldview would expand.
- We would intellectually and spiritually become closer to God.
- We would learn more about God's plan for each and every one of us.
- We would believe in the wholeness and unity of life.
- We would become more accepting of other people, traditions, and cultures.
- We would learn more deeply about ourselves and the nature of life itself.

Nevertheless, for a great many people in today's frantically changing world, it is just too hard to stop and ponder about anything beyond their own basic duties, responsibilities, difficulties, and personal relationships that are so essential to daily life. But if you are one of those mindful individuals who are willing to look beyond your everyday mundane existence, enhance your thinking process, broaden your outlook on the world, and question why certain things happen, then this book is for you.

Chapter I
THE GRAND DESIGN

What is it about the night sky that expands the senses and appeals to the innermost soul? Why do our hearts beat faster, our veins flow quicker, and our emotions grow stronger during the full moon? Perhaps a potential answer can be found embedded within the ancient spiritual writings of our collective past. As one of the earliest known historical documents in the world, the Hebrew Bible, recognized by modern Christians as the Old Testament, accurately records much of the early human experience and can provide a great many clues. But what does astrology have to do with it? As you shall find, all these questions, and more, will be addressed here.

When viewed without interference by clouds or unnatural light, the pure and unobstructed night sky is clean, intense, and invigorating to the senses. When illuminated only by the broad path of the moon and the fine light of the stars, the craftsmanship of God's mighty hand can easily be seen and felt. And with just a small understanding of the motions of the planets in the solar system, they too will come sharply into focus.

On some occasions, you can watch the splendid descent of Venus moving downward toward the western horizon shortly after sunset. At other times, you might watch Mercury brilliantly rising just before sunrise as the morning star, or perhaps the brilliant path of Jupiter as it crosses the midheaven of the night sky.

It hardly comes as a surprise, then, that the vast celestial patterns have been studied by human beings since the beginning of time. The careful observation of planetary movements became one of the first techniques used by early man in an effort to understand God's grand plan. Today, we are just as compelled to ask, as our ancestors surely must have asked, these two important questions: Who or what could have placed the moving planets and the vast array of celestial lights into the heavens, in such a designated and perfect arrangement, had it not been the mighty hand of God himself? Who or what could have persuaded humans to gather and apply such an immense quantity of spiritual knowledge from those compelling nightly patterns, had it not been the same mighty God?

Toward this end, the practice of astrology is based, first and foremost, upon a fundamental concordance with the ways of heaven. The understanding of how celestial patterns are closely related to human events permits us to develop a deeper understanding of God's will here on Earth. Life without the knowledge of astrology becomes much more chaotic. Clearly, the information obtained from the study of astrology allows us to formulate a more appropriate set of behaviors within our own personal lives. As one astrologer succinctly notes, "Similar to weather forecasting . . . we watch so we can prepare our response to future conditions in an effort to ensure our comfort, prosperity, safety, and security" (Kochunas 2016). Consequently, the more we watch, the more we can learn, and the better we become equipped to respond to the foremost challenges of life.

THE HOLY BIBLE

In this book, we will review many sections of the Holy Bible that support the use of astrology to assist mankind in the quest for knowledge from and about God. All biblical references are obtained from the Authorized King James version, unless otherwise specified. In essence, the Bible's supporting evidence for astrology is mainly derived from one fundamental and transparent belief: the confident acceptance that there is a purposeful creation and arrangement to the heavens. This fundamental belief is nicely expressed here by the Institute for Creation Research: "Evidently the stars were arranged by God to 'signify' something to those on earth, not just scattered evenly or randomly around in space. God even named the stars and their constellations" (Morris 2006).

Most religious thinkers accept the basic conviction that the heavens and stars were purposefully created by God. This belief was clearly revealed when Isaiah commanded:

> *Lift up your eyes on high, and behold who hath created these things, that bringeth out their host by number: he calleth them all by names by the greatness of his might, for that he is strong in power; not one faileth* (Isaiah 40:26).

Indeed, Amos told us to *"Seek him that maketh the seven stars and Orion"* (Amos 5:8). The same message was confirmed by Job, when he wrote that God specifically made certain stars known to us as Arcturus, Orion, and Pleiades (Job 9:9). Job repeated that message again later when writing of God, *"By his spirit he hath garnished the heavens"* (Job 26:13).

Without a doubt, there are numerous sections of the old Hebrew Bible portraying the belief that the heavens and stars were purposely created as part of a grand celestial design administered by God. It is quite probable that most of the other ancient religions of the world have at their core a similar type of creation narrative, each one embodying a relationship between the cosmos and humanity, and envisioned against the huge backdrop and starry display of the heavens. The close correspondence among planets in the sky, the arrangement of the stars, and patterns of events on Earth was part of this discovery. We shall learn that astrology thus became a natural and intrinsic part of the search for meaning and understanding of God throughout the ages, and we shall explore how some of this early background applies to us living in the world today.

EXPERIENCING A GRAND CELESTIAL DESIGN

As humans relentlessly searched for meaning in the sky, a fascination with astrology seems to have occurred simultaneously in many of the earliest known cultures around the world. There developed a universal and multicultural acceptance by humanity that a sense of meaningfulness in life could be derived only from God, either from a series of multiple or pagan "gods" that appeared in earlier cultures, or from the monotheistic Hebrew God worshiped by the ancient Jewish people. A deep feeling of significance was revealed to mankind from the night sky and the heavens above through close observation and study of the constantly advancing planetary movements.

Some of the earliest known surviving records on the origins and beginnings of astrology may be connected to the ancient stone megaliths and huge earthen mounds erected during the Neolithic period. The earliest historical sites likely combining both religious and astronomical or astrological overtones date in the range of 8000 BCE to 3000 BCE. These archaeological sites include the famous Stonehenge in England, as well as many other early megalithic sites. Fascinating archaeological examples have been found in many diverse locations of the world, including Armenia, Germany, Malta, Egypt, and the Negev Desert near the Palestine area (Campion 2008). Researchers have proven that many of these stone monuments directly correspond to celestial patterns of movement formed by the sun and moon (Hawkins 1965; Mitchell 1982).

Being in close proximity to Mesopotamia and Egypt, where some of the earliest astrological writings have been discovered, Palestine and the ancestral Hebrews were profoundly linked to the initial use of astrology as a means to derive meaning from the sky. It makes perfect sense to now discover a claim that has long been immersed within the ancient historical literature, the simple statement that monotheistic astrology was invented by the Hebrew people. This information was recorded in the first century CE by Josephus, one of the most renowned of early Jewish historians.

Josephus describes Seth, who was the son of Adam, as a man who esteemed God most highly, and his children are glowingly portrayed as the most virtuous of men. Josephus explicitly writes that Seth and his children "were the inventors of that particular sort of wisdom which is concerned with the heavenly bodies and their order" (Josephus, trans. Whiston, 1737). Josephus goes on to state that Abraham, who is recognized as the forefather and progenitor of the Hebrew people, was traditionally known as the first astrologer to present to the world the original concept that planets in their celestial paths were used as holy agents of the one true God (Josephus trans., Whiston 1737; Campion 2012).

Knowing that this information comes down to us from ancient Hebrew records, these statements are highly likely to be historically accurate. We understand that Abraham was born in the Chaldean city of Ur, which is located in ancient Sumer, where astrology was well known and commonly practiced. According to the scriptures, Abraham was seventy-five years old when he left Ur (see Genesis 12:1–5). "When he obeyed God's command to emigrate with his family to the land of Canaan, he must have taken along with him the Chaldean understanding of the heavens" (Dixon 1987, 8). But by moving away, Abraham clearly rejected the antagonistic belief in multiple gods demonstrated by the Chaldean culture. Abraham went on to embrace a new tradition of monotheistic astrology in his adopted land, which he then passed down to his descendants.

Many modern religious scholars confirm these ancient beginnings. One Christian theologian recently wrote: "The fact that astrology was previously an integral part of both Judaism and Christianity is irrefutable" (Detweiler 2012). Another contemporary theologian, himself a rabbi, agrees: "The basic philosophical thrust of astrology derives from the conviction that the human being, God, and the universe are in some way a unity; that man and universe, if you will, both swim in the sea of space-time whose substance is God" (Dobin 2012).

Archaeologists continue to find indisputable, concrete, physical evidence with clear depictions of the celestial zodiac buried within the ruins of many ancient Hebrew synagogues. For instance, the Hammoth-Tiberius synagogue, discovered on the western shore of the Sea of Galilee, contains an ancient stone zodiac palpably embedded in the floor of the synagogue. The ruins at another Jewish synagogue at Zippori (or Sepphoris), in lower Galilee, contain a mosaic of the zodiac as it correlates with the months of the Hebrew calendar. And again on the floor of a third ancient synagogue at Ein Gedi, located near the Dead Sea, archaeologists discovered a list of the twelve zodiac signs that depicted a direct correspondence with the months of the Hebrew calendar (Detweiler 2012).

Indeed, the Dead Sea scrolls, found hidden in the desert at Qumran between 1945 and 1952, are known as "the earliest primary sources of books of the Bible" (Jacobus 2009). Scholars agree that these manuscripts, which were written in the Hebrew and Aramaic languages, are dated sometime around the third century BCE, up until the mid-first century CE. One of these scrolls has been titled by researchers as the *Zodiac Calendar* (scroll numbered 4Q318) and clearly portrays the astrological calendar and other essential Hebrew cultural details surrounding the practice of astrology.

Another astonishing resource can be found within the Dead Sea scroll titled the *Zodiacal Physiognomy* (scroll numbered 4Q186). This ancient Hebrew manuscript actually consists of an astrological textbook or handbook detailing how the signs of the zodiac are inextricably related to the facial and bodily characteristics of individuals (Popovic 2007). Clearly then, these ancient scrolls and historical documents should cast no doubt whatsoever that a close link existed between the ancient Hebrew people and the cultural practice of astrology.

A moment ago, we mentioned that these scrolls are considered "primary sources." Just what does "primary" mean? Written in the ancient languages, the texts are unadulterated and unchanged since their original writing. Their historical significance is absolutely astounding, for the scrolls have never been previously translated or edited in any way. That they identify an unreservedly strong influence between astrology and Jewish life is frankly indisputable.

Accordingly, we should also ask ourselves this next important question: Why was it necessary to hide the Dead Sea scrolls in the first place? We will surely come back to this essential question later on in the book. But for now, let us say with complete certainty that the manuscripts and archaeological sites mentioned here are just a few of the many fine historical artifacts and documents that demonstrate an overwhelming abundance of physical evidence and irrefutably prove these basic underlying concepts. The practice of astrology clearly had deep religious significance ever since the time of Abraham at the beginning of the monotheistic Hebrew culture. And the Dead Sea scrolls have proven beyond any doubt that the systematic practice of astrology within the Hebrew culture continued throughout the centuries immediately before and surrounding the life and death of Jesus Christ.

THE POWER OF SEVEN

Due to this solid physical evidence, there can be absolutely no doubt that astrology played a fundamental role in the early Jewish faith in God. By what other means can we determine this statement is true? Does other evidence still exist? It is actually quite easy to find a great deal of superb astrological symbolism immersed within many of the traditional Hebrew rituals.

One highly notable example of astrological symbolism is the original sacred menorah, the Jewish candelabra holding seven lights, which, according to Josephus, specifically symbolized the light of the seven visible planets (Campion 2012). These planets include Mercury, Venus, Mars, Jupiter, and Saturn, plus the sun and the moon. Note that the original definition for the word "planets" simply meant "moving bodies" against the predominantly fixed celestial background (Holden 2006, 13). As viewed from Earth, the planetary bodies in apparent motion thus included the sun and moon. And as we have seen earlier, these same seven moving bodies were termed "the seven stars" in Amos 5:8.

A highly detailed description on the construction of the holy menorah with seven lights can be found in Exodus 25. Please bear in mind that the original sacred menorah is now only employed for religious ceremony in temples and is not the same commonly used menorah of nine lamps that is found in homes during the more modern Jewish celebration of Chanukah (United with Israel 2015). The original practice that identified the number 7 as sacred is found in Genesis 1:1 through Genesis 2:3, whereby God created heaven and Earth in six days, and on the seventh day ended his work, rested, and blessed and sanctified the seventh day as the Sabbath.

Again, the evidence cannot be disputed. Moses was divinely instructed to follow the design of the heavens when developing the rituals and patterns of the Hebrew religion: *"And look that thou make them after their pattern, which was shewed thee in the mount"* (Exodus 25:40). The same statement is repeated by Paul, a devout Jew before converting to Christianity, in his letter to the Hebrew people: *"There are priests that offer gifts according to the law: who serve under the example and shadow of the heavenly things, as Moses was admonished by God when he was about to make the tabernacle: for See, saith he, that thou make all things according to the pattern shewed to thee in the mount"* (Hebrews 8:4–5).

There is other written evidence that Moses was an astrologer, found in the works of at least three different histories of antiquity (including that of the third-century Christian historian Origen). Those writers ascertained that "Moses himself had been 'skillful in the same arts'" as his astrological forefathers (Hegedus 2007, 205). This celestial knowledge of astrology must have assisted Moses greatly when transferring the divine pattern of the heavens into Hebrew religious ritual.

The practice of seven is still celebrated today, as people in cultures worldwide measure time and divide the week into seven days that are named after the seven visible planets. Although partially obscured in the English language, the modern names for the seven days of the week follow the old Teutonic and Roman names for the planets ruling each day, as follows:

Sunday	Sun day
Monday	Moon day
Tuesday	Tiew's day (Mars)
Wednesday	Woden's day (Mercury)
Thursday	Thor's day (Jupiter)
Friday	Freya's day (Venus)
Saturday	Saturn day

(Holden 2006)

Much is found in the scripture identifying the number 7. Emanating from God's hand as the number of visible planets, the number 7 also represents God's will brought down to Earth from the celestial sphere. The following list gives just a partial example of the holy power of seven, including many common rules Moses laid out for the Hebrew people, as instructed by God.

> The Sabbath day: *"Six days shall work be done: but the seventh day is the Sabbath of rest, an holy convocation"* (Leviticus 23:3).

> The feast of unleavened bread: *"Seven days ye must eat unleavened bread . . . Ye shall offer an offering made by fire unto the Lord seven days: in the seventh day is an holy convocation"* (Leviticus 23:6–8).

> The feast of harvest: This feast is celebrated after *"seven Sabbaths shall be complete,"* from the day of bringing in the sheaf of wheat (Leviticus 23:15).

> Numerous other holy celebrations: The feast of trumpets, the holy day of atonement, and the feast of the tabernacles all occurred during the seventh month and included seven days of offerings (Leviticus 23:23–44).

The year of rest: *"In the seventh year shall be a Sabbath of rest unto the land, a Sabbath for the Lord: thou shalt neither sow thy field nor prune thy vineyard"* (Leviticus 25:4).

The year of jubilee: *"And thou shalt number seven Sabbaths of years unto thee, seven times seven years; and the space of the seven Sabbaths of years shall be unto thee forty and nine years. Then thou shalt cause the trumpet of the jubilee to sound on the tenth day of the seventh month. . . . For it is the jubilee; it shall be holy unto you"* (Leviticus 25:8–12).

The predictions of Joseph: Seven years of plenty, followed by seven years of famine throughout the land of Egypt *"because the thing is established by God"* (Genesis 41:28–32).

The fall of Jericho: Seven priests and seven trumpets preceded the ark of the covenant during the siege of Jericho. The siege lasted seven days, and on the seventh day at the seventh blow of the trumpet, the walls of Jericho fell (Joshua 6:1–20).

Seven Psalms are attributed to David (Psalms 2, 16, 32, 41, 69, 95, 109).

We could go on and on. Seven is said to be the number of completeness and perfection (both physical and spiritual) when tied to the creation (Wellman 2014a). Clearly the number 7 follows God's divine word, as seen in the words above stated by Joseph, *"because the thing is established by God."* Accordingly, seven heavens were recognized by the Jews, each heaven pertaining to one of the seven planets, of which the seventh heaven was the place of God and was represented by the planet Saturn, the seventh visible planet.

THE MEANING OF TWELVE

Symbolizing the grand and sacred celestial design created by God, the number 12 is another number that is frequently repeated throughout the Old Testament. The number 12 represents both the number of lunar months in a Hebrew religious year and the twelve ancient signs or divisions of the celestial zodiac. That there are twelve sons of Jacob is not just a mere coincidence. The scriptural passage in Genesis 49:1–28 goes on to depict the dominant characteristics of each of the twelve sons in much-greater detail. Here it is highly significant that the descriptions of Jacob's twelve sons closely match the traditional archetypes pertaining to the twelve astrological signs of the zodiac.

Upon entering the promised land of Canaan, Moses divided the Hebrew people into twelve tribes. While proclaiming the sacred inheritance for the children of Israel, Moses sectioned the land into twelve regions. The last chapter of Ezekiel pronounced that under the sovereignty of God, the land allotment for Israel should follow twelve discrete divisions.

When crossing the Jordan River, Joshua commanded that twelve stones be set

> *"here the feet of the priests which bare the ark of the covenant stood: and they are there to this day. . . . And he spake unto the children of Israel, saying, When your children ask their fathers in time to come, saying what mean these stones? Then ye shall let your children know, saying Israel came over this Jordan on dry land. For the Lord your God dried up the waters of Jordan from before you. . . . That all the people of the earth might know the hand of the Lord, that it is mighty: that ye might fear the Lord your God for ever* (Joshua 4:9, 21–24).

Here the twelve stones of the Jordan were found to carry a very important message for future generations. It follows that the number 12 shall be used as a remembrance for the mighty hand of God and as a symbol of God's power and authority, for all of the generations of man, both present and future.

An ancient Hebrew ritual practices placing twelve cakes of unleavened bread *"upon the pure table before the Lord"* within the holy temple (Leviticus 24:5–6). The traditional Jewish calendar is divided into twelve lunar months. The hours of daylight between sunrise and sunset are customarily numbered twelve, and even today the daily clock is divided into twelve hours.

NUMBERS IN THE NEW TESTAMENT

The numbers 7 and 12 are frequently repeated many times over and over within the New Testament, and the gospels often tell of the twelve apostles of Jesus. Here it is noteworthy that a book written by the devout Christian astrologer, psychic, and seer Jeane Dixon describes a recurring religious vision regarding the twelve apostles of Christ. Similar to the twelve sons of Jacob in the Old Testament, she writes that the unique personalities of the twelve apostles represent the twelve different signs of the celestial zodiac. Dixon states that she received this revelation during prayer while faithfully attending church and goes on to write many interesting details supporting her vision (Dixon 1987).

Again, we see the same numbers repeated. Jesus was twelve years old when he first astonished Jewish scholars with deep religious understanding (Luke 2:42–47). Jesus healed a woman who had an issue of blood for twelve years, an event that occurred on the same day that he raised a man's twelve-year-old daughter from the dead (Matthew 8:40–56). Immediately following this event, Jesus called his twelve apostles together to give them power over all manner of devils and disease, and sent them forth to preach and heal (Luke 9:1–2).

Matthew identifies the seven parables of Jesus (Matthew 13) and lists the seven woes or judgments of the Pharisees (Matthew 23). In his letter to Hebrews, Paul uses seven titles to refer to Christ (Hebrews 1–12). Jesus is further described in the midst of seven golden candlesticks, where *"he had in his right hand seven stars. . . . And his countenance was as the sun shineth in strength"* (Revelation 1:16).

The Revelation of John goes on to describe the seven churches, seven seals, seven trumpets, seven bowls, twelve gates, twelve angels, and twelve pearls of heaven. New Jerusalem is built with walls that are 144 cubits high (a multiple of twelve times twelve), measures 12,000 furloughs in length, and is built on twelve foundations made of twelve different precious stones (Revelation 21).

Jesus told John to write of these things he has seen:

> *The mystery of the seven stars which thou sawest in my right hand, and the seven golden candlesticks. The seven stars are the angels of the seven churches: and the seven candlesticks which thou sawest are the seven churches* (Revelation 1:20).

Furthermore, we find that the same number 7 represents *"the seven Spirits of God sent forth into all the earth"* (Revelation 5:6). Yet could the repeated numbers in all of these events be due to mere coincidence?

DIVINE SYMBOLISM

According to the Holy Bible, we believe that Moses wrote the books of Genesis through Deuteronomy between 1446 and 1406 BCE. These books constitute the first five books at the beginning of the Hebrew Bible or Old Testament. Indeed, scholars identify twelve historical books in the Old Testament (Wellman 2014b).

The Hebrew Bible itself remains a superbly preserved historical document that spans a great many centuries and is thought to cover the entire historical period starting with the time of Abraham, ca. 2000 BCE, down to the beginning of the Roman conquest of the Mediterranean world, which occurred in approximately 200 BCE (Noble 2002a).

In the examples shown above, we can visualize how Moses described God's original creation and design of the universe. Through the symbolism of the seven visible planets and the twelve signs of the celestial zodiac, Moses then translated the grand design of God's creation into discrete patterns and rituals for religious and human practice. By utilizing the divinely derived numbers 7 and 12, Moses brought the divinity of God's celestial design down to Earth for use in human activity.

We know that the numbers 7 and 12 are continually repeated throughout both the Old and New Testaments. Accordingly, it is imperative to remember that *"this is the interpretation of the thing . . . God hath numbered thy kingdom"* (Daniel 5:26) in a deeply significant way. As Luke has said, *"even the very hairs of your head are all numbered"* (Luke 12:7). Consequently, the frequent repetition of the specific numbers 7 and 12 must have been done quite deliberately. Meant to signify something of great importance, the repetition can hardly be ignored.

By now, the skeptical reader may be thinking that these repeated numbers could still be just coincidence. What if the numbers were not designed to indicate celestial correspondence but represented something else entirely? Please keep on reading. Even more astonishing proof is yet to come in the following chapters.

It is not my intention to provide a review of every single reference to astrology within the Bible. I simply wish to demonstrate that the divine order and supreme beauty of the cosmos can be perfectly described and profoundly recognized through the study of astrology. It is my sincere hope that readers will realize that astrology is essentially derived from, and continues to follow, the divine order created by the hand of God. Perhaps we can then work to develop the use of astrology as a tool to assist in the fundamental understanding of ourselves and our continuing relationship with God.

By opening our minds to astrology, we can allow a deeper understanding of the universe itself, we can recognize the true wonders of God's divine plan for each and every person, and we can hope to obtain greater individual access to the spiritually profound riches derived only from God. Astrology thus becomes the true and amazing evidence of God's will working in the life of every individual. This evidence can be discovered through a study of the heavens and forms an indispensable foundation in the belief system adopted by every astrologer today.

Chapter II:
Foundations of Astrology:
THE HEBREW BIBLE AND
OLD TESTAMENT

Beginning in the very first chapter, the Hebrew Bible and Old Testament teaches us that astrology is an intrinsic part of God's divine plan:

> In the beginning, God created the heaven and the earth" (Genesis 1:1). "And God said, Let there be lights in the firmament of the heaven to divide the day from the night; and let them be for signs, and for seasons, and for days, and years . . . And God made two great lights; the greater light to rule the day, and the lesser light to rule the night: He made the stars also (Genesis 1:14, 16).

We immediately understand the meaning of the "lights" to be the sun, which is called the greater light, and the moon, which is called the lesser light. But what did Moses indicate by also calling the lights to be "signs" in the heavens? Signs for what purpose?

We know that the reference to the seasons coincides with many of the basic needs of agriculture. Humans throughout ancient history have used the movements and angles of the sun across the sky to designate appropriate planting and harvest seasons, as well as the movements of the moon through the divisions of the zodiac to determine religious calendars and to determine the best timing for human activity (Lehman 2011, 16–17). The signs, or divisions of the sky into the zodiac, were discovered and developed to track the apparent movements of the sun, moon, and planets through the heavens in a rational and orderly way. The names of the zodiac signs correspond with the original twelve constellations bearing the same names.

Even today, many experienced and knowledgeable gardeners will tell you the best zodiac signs and phases of the moon that unfailingly produce superior results when planting or harvesting a garden. Numerous human activities just seem to prosper when initiated under the best zodiacal signs and phases of the moon for that particular activity (Pyle and Reese 1993). This information has been known, followed, and put into practical use throughout the millennium before Christ by the early peoples of Sumer and Mesopotamia, as well as by the ancient Hebrew people.

THE ZODIACAL SIGNS

It is not a coincidence that the twelve divisions of the zodiac, the names of which astrologers still use today, are also called the "signs" of the zodiac. The early Hebrew people followed the movements of the sun, moon, and visible planets throughout the celestial zodiac in a framework of profound religious meaning. The zodiacal signs were originally named after the actual visual constellations or groupings of stars as they appeared from Earth more than 3,000 years ago. Later, due to the constant precession or apparent backward movement of the stars, the zodiac signs were refined into specific mathematical divisions based upon the movement of the sun along the ecliptic, which is the observed path of the sun as it appears to move around the Earth.

While they take their names from the constellations, the zodiacal signs are determined entirely by the annual orbit of the Earth around the sun. The four seasons are based on the tilt of the Earth on its axis at an angle about 23 degrees. Accordingly, the zodiac signs are precisely derived from the equinox and solstice points that divide the year into four seasons. While the seasons once corresponded with the constellations arising on the horizon at dawn, they no longer do so because of the slow but continuous apparent backward movement of the stars. This precessional drifting of the stars is itself a result of a slight but noticeable wobble of the Earth in its own orbit around the sun.

The geometry of the zodiac signs is concisely explained here by astrologer Glenn Perry, PhD:

> The sign is simply the angle of the earth's orbital position relative to the vernal equinox, nothing more. . . . Again, constellations have nothing to do with the tropical zodiac. These made up star groups were initially used by ancient tribesmen for determining the timing of seasonal processes. . . . Zodiacal signs and tropical constellations are completely different things despite their sharing the same names. . . . Whereas constellations are arbitrary groupings of stars

that have no actual boundaries, zodiac signs are precise geometric angles derived from the equinoctial and solstice points (Perry 2016).

During the second century BCE, it became increasingly evident that the constellations rising on the horizon no longer matched the geometrically derived zodiacal signs. However, it was not until the second century CE that a tropical zodiac independent of the constellations was developed by the famous Greek astronomer named Ptolemy. Nevertheless, "the fact that the signs retained the name of the constellations to which they once corresponded continues to cause confusion to this day" (Perry 2016).

The natural zodiac begins in Aries at the exact moment of the spring equinox (when the length of daylight precisely equals the length of darkness). Even though the zodiac signs no longer perfectly match the visual constellations for which they were originally named, their location on the solar ecliptic, and their relationship to the points of the solar solstice and equinox, retain enormous importance and are extremely relevant today.

During the Middle Ages, the Copernican revolution allowed us to understand that the sun does not really revolve around the Earth. Yet this knowledge does not change the mathematical divisions of the zodiac nor the apparent movements of celestial bodies as seen from Earth. Regardless of the understanding that the Earth actually revolves around the sun, the observed motions of the sun and planets of the solar system along the path of the ecliptic follow the same cyclic motions that have always been seen. The Copernican revolution did not alter the meaning and usefulness of astrology. More details on this subject will be forthcoming in a later chapter.

JUST WHAT IS A SIGN?

A sign is "any omen or miraculous occurrence" (Funk & Wagnalls 1984), or perhaps a symbol or marker of some kind, which gives information and refers or points to something of extreme importance. Moses would not have used the word "sign" in the verses of Genesis unless it is extremely important information for humanity. When ideas are very important, the Bible tends to repeat the same ideas, words, or phrases over and over again. Later on, in the New Testament, we shall see how particularly important this word becomes when an angel from God appears before the shepherds in the fields and announces the birth of Christ the Savior:

> And this shall be a sign unto you; Ye shall find the babe wrapped in swaddling clothes, lying in a manger (Luke 2:12).

It is of great consequence that the word "sign" came down through the ages also representing the twelve divisions of the celestial zodiac. Notice that the English word "sign" is the root for such words as significant, signify, signal, and signet. Thus, we find that the early Hebrews, when writing in Genesis, used a word that was later translated to describe not only the celestial divisions of day and night, but also to mean any extremely meaningful symbol emanating from God.

Later in Psalms, the Bible once again speaks of the moon, lights, and stars as part of God's purposeful creation of the heavens:

> *When I consider thy heavens, the work of thy fingers, the moon and the stars, which thou hast ordained* (Psalms 8:3);

> *To Him that made great lights: for his mercy endureth for ever: The sun to rule by day: for his mercy endureth for ever: The moon and the stars to rule by night: for his mercy endureth for ever* (Psalms 136:7–9).

Here and in the Genesis passages mentioned earlier, the text of the Bible repeats the word "rule" when referring to the sun and moon's dominion over the sky of the day and the sky of the night. To rule is to have control, power, authority, or guidance over something (Funk & Wagnalls 1984). It follows that astrologers view the sun and the moon as having the most-powerful influences in the horoscopes of human beings. But the lights and other astrological influences never actually force people to do anything at all; we always have the free will given to us by God. And since God created the sun and moon and stars in the first place, anything guided by the lights must also be planned according to God's will. According to the text of the Bible, the lights were clearly placed in the heavens to be signs, and therefore a means to provide help, assurance, protection, guidance, and assistance for mankind.

Historically, the writer of Judges, traditionally thought to be Samuel, states: *"They fought from heaven; the stars in their courses fought against Sisera"* (Judges 5:20), thereby assisting Israel to win its battles against Sisera. Indeed, for Christians, the greatest everlasting help of all time came to us from heaven and was given to man by God. The Christ and Savior of mankind was predicted by Moses when he said, *"there shall come a Star out of Jacob"* (Numbers 24:17). And we know that the wise men from the east followed the Star of Bethlehem,

> *Saying, where is he that is born King of the Jews? For we have seen his star in the east, and are come to worship him* (Matthew 2:2).

Thus, we clearly find a great deal of undisputed evidence that the stars were used as signs from God. Numerous sections in the Bible distinctly indicate that the sun, moon, and stars were placed in the heavens not only to provide physical light for mankind, but also to provide a means of spiritual guidance, holy assistance, and a form of sacred light. People today can undoubtedly learn these same lessons that were given to our forebears and recorded in the Bible by Moses, Samuel, Matthew, and other ancient biblical writers.

THE TRADITIONAL UNDERSTANDING OF WISDOM

Biblical historians agree that before and during the time of Christ, astrologers were traditionally known as "magi" or "wise men" (Showalter 2001; Papini 1970; Holden 2006). Given that honorable designation, astrologers were inherently thought to be men of much wisdom and great understanding. The use of the word "wise" in the description of astrologers is in itself quite remarkable. The attainment of wisdom is one of the overriding themes in the book of Proverbs and may perhaps be summarized in the following verses:

> To know wisdom and instruction; to perceive the words of understanding; to receive the instruction of wisdom, justice, and judgment, and equity; to give subtlety to the simple, to the young man knowledge and discretion. A wise man will hear, and will increase learning; a man of understanding shall attain wise counsels (Proverbs 1:2–5).

Several other passages in Proverbs attest to the spiritual origins, importance, and character of wisdom. It was believed that all wisdom comes from God (Harrelson 1964). Moreover, the theme of attaining wisdom and understanding is also repeated in Job, where it is theoretically asked:

> But where shall wisdom be found? And where is the place of understanding? Man knoweth not the price thereof; neither is it found in the hand of the living (Job 28:12–13).

Job continues by stating:

> It cannot be gotten for gold, neither shall silver be weighed for the price thereof (Job 28:15).

God understandeth the way thereof, and he knoweth the price thereof (Job 28:23).

And unto man he said, Behold, the fear of the Lord, that is wisdom; and to depart from evil is understanding (Job 28:28).

Here in these passages, we learn of the tremendous worth and importance being given to the attainment of wisdom. To be considered a wise man is a great achievement of exceptional value. Consequently, use of the particular term "wise man" to describe an astrologer signifies all of the traits described above: an extraordinary mental and spiritual accomplishment, the departure from evil, and a deeper understanding of the ways of God.

A man of achievement among the Hebrews, Rabbi Ibn Ezra justified the use of those words. In 1148 CE, he wrote a book he called *The Beginning of Wisdom*, which became a basic textbook for astrologers for centuries. Written in the traditional Arabic style of astrology, this book was copied many times over and translated from the Hebrew language into multiple other languages. With the very first line of his book, Ibn Ezra, a devout monotheistic Jew, stated the following: "The beginning of wisdom is the fear of God, for it is the instruction. . . . So, here I shall begin to interpret the laws of the heavens according to the rules as practiced by the ancients, generation after generation" (Ibn Ezra 1998, translated by Epstein, 1).

Who were "the ancients" according to Ibn Ezra? Going back so many generations, we understand Ibn Ezra to mean his ancient Hebrew ancestors, certainly the wise men of old. Clearly, as the beginning statement in the premier astrological textbook of the times, this statement makes it absolutely clear that astrologers knew that the source of their wisdom, knowledge, and understanding came directly from God.

AN IMPORTANT QUALIFICATION

A definitive distinction must be made between astrology, which is the *study and understanding* of the movements of the stars and planets, particularly as related to human events, as opposed to the *religious worship* of the stars or planets. The religious worship of the planets, such as the religious practice found in ancient Babylon or Chaldea, was a blatant form of idolatry and a type of pagan religion and obviously does not apply to astrology in and of itself. Thus, the wisdom of astrology is not the same thing as pagan worship of the planets; they are two distinctly different things. A strong division clearly exists between astrology and pagan idolatry, a division that must be deeply emphasized and made completely transparent and unambiguous. Hebrew astrologers and biblical wise men ultimately studied and learned about God's creation by following the patterns and movements of the planets, but they certainly did not worship them like the pagan Babylonians did.

As a field of study today, anyone of any belief may become an astrologer. Just as professionals from any field of study, such as counselors, psychologists, teachers, physicians, or chemists, may be Jewish, Christian, Islamic, pagan, or any other religion, so it is true with modern-day astrologers. It bears repeating: Astrology is the study or wisdom of the stars as related to human events, and astrology is *not* a religion. The early Hebrew astrologers described in the Bible always maintained their Jewish heritage and celebrated a belief in their one true Hebrew God. Also in my own mind, the great orderly creation of the heavens that is so aptly demonstrated by astrology can lead to no other final conclusion but a strong belief in God.

A SEPARATE CLASS

According to the writings by Charles Foster Kent, a biblical scholar who wrote a treatise in 1896, the wise men were a separate class of Hebrew teachers who "labored so unobtrusively that their work has been almost unnoticed. They spoke in private to the individual, and not in public to the nation," advising kings and all classes of people in ancient Israel. Perhaps for these reasons, there has been very little written about the wise men. "Everything that concerned the ordinary man commanded their attention. They were equally ready with practical advice concerning anything, from the purchase of a farm to a man's duty to his God" (Kent 1908).

Apparently, then, ancient astrologers or wise men primarily worked behind the scenes within Hebrew society. The practical advice provided by astrologers thus not only concerns the timing of farming activities, but also religious activities and every other type of human event. Here I am reminded of the frequently repeated passages from Ecclesiastics, of which the first two verses are recorded below. From these scriptures, we learn that the timing of every single human activity clearly occurs according to God's impeccable will:

> To everything is a season, and a time to every purpose under heaven: A time to be born, a time to die; a time to plant, and a time to pluck up that which is planted (Ecclesiastics 3:1–2).

We can only conclude that during early biblical tradition, the wise men were astrologers who were well known for their studious and laborious attentions to time, season, and purpose. They applied their priceless wisdom and knowledge of the stars and planetary movements toward the practical matters of mankind, as well as toward teaching about the holy matters of God.

PSALMS 19

Very few passages in the Bible are more poignant or more explicit in clarifying the understanding of astrology as a fundamental part of God's plan, than in the scriptures found in Psalms 19:

> *The heavens declare the glory of God; and the firmament sheweth his handiwork. Day unto day uttereth speech, and night unto night sheweth knowledge. There is no speech nor language where their voice is not heard* (Psalms 19:1–3).

These passages declare that night after night, the heavens and the stars illuminate the glory of God and bring forth nightly knowledge from God even to the far corners of the Earth. What else can the nightly knowledge shown by the heavens be, if it is not the knowledge of astrology? Thus, we must consider astrology to be the enactment of God's word to mankind though a study of the stars and celestial movements. Psalms 19 then continues:

> *The law of the Lord is perfect, converting the soul: the testimony of the Lord is sure, making wise the simple. The statutes of the Lord are right, rejoicing the heart: the commandment of the Lord is pure, enlightening the eyes. . . . Moreover by them is thy servant warned: and in keeping of them there is great reward* (Psalms 19:7–7, 11).

These scriptures proclaim that the testimony of the heavens is pure and perfect, is heard worldwide, converts the soul, and provides great knowledge to make the simple man "wise." Once again, please take note of the word "wise" repeated here. The passages confirm that this nightly knowledge comes directly from God, rejoices the heart, and enlightens the eyes. Could there be a more apt and fitting description of astrology? By viewing the night sky, the wise man obtains more perfect knowledge from God, is further enlightened, and develops even greater wisdom by doing this activity. In addition, great rewards may be achieved.

DANIEL AND THE WISE MEN

A great deal of information regarding the background of the wise men can be discovered in the Book of Daniel. During the time that King Nebuchadnezzar of Babylon had conquered Jerusalem, in or about 537 BCE, Daniel wrote that he spent time in Nebuchadnezzar's court as an astrologer and wise man. Daniel and his companions are shown to be pious Jews who are protected by God and endowed with wisdom surpassing even that of the Babylonian astrologers and wise men (Coogan and Towner 2001).

In the second year of his reign, King Nebuchadnezzar wished to have the wise men of the court interpret a dream:

> *Then the king commanded to call the magicians, and the astrologers, and the sorcerers, and the Chaldeans, for to shew the king his dreams. So they came and stood before the king* (Daniel 2:2).

But the dream had been forgotten by the king and he could not repeat it, thus making the task impossible. The other wise men were unable to interpret the dream, at which point it was written:

> *And the decree went forth that the wise men should be slain; and they sought Daniel and his fellows to be slain. . . . Then Daniel went in, and desired of the king that he would give him time, and that he would show the king the interpretation. Then Daniel went to his house, and made the thing known to . . . his companions: That they would desire mercies of the God of heaven concerning this secret; that Daniel and his fellows should not perish with the rest of the wise men of Babylon* (Daniel 2:13, 16–18).

Because we know that Daniel was not a magician, sorcerer, or from Chaldea, these passages explicitly relate that Daniel was a wise man and an astrologer. King Nebuchadnezzar did give Daniel extra time, and the secret was then revealed to Daniel that same night in a vision from God. As Daniel thanked God for the vision, which saved his life, he said that God *"giveth wisdom into the wise, and knowledge to them that know understanding"* (Daniel 2:21), once more confirming Daniel's role as a wise man and astrologer.

We see that as an astrologer, Daniel had already ascertained much wisdom, knowledge, and understanding, but his knowledge alone was not good enough to interpret the forgotten and unknown dream of Nebuchadnezzar. The greater wisdom of God was needed and was then revealed to Daniel through God's blessing, which saved his life.

A vitally important message shown in these passages is that God provided an exceptional blessing to Daniel, who was known to be a wise man and astrologer.

And in a similar manner (to be more fully discussed in another chapter), God later blessed the wise men who traveled from the East to worship the newborn baby Jesus.

Consequently, as seen in Psalms 19 and here with Daniel, the knowledge of astrology can be a vital and intrinsic part of God's plan for all of us, too, as we attempt to learn God's path within our own lives. A finer, more accurate understanding of this path can be assisted through a deeper understanding of astrology.

ARE THERE ANY BIBLICAL CITATIONS CONDEMNING ASTROLOGY?

Persons claiming that a condemnation of astrology is found within the Old Testament have named certain passages that will now be briefly examined. I shall prove beyond a doubt that any condemnations of astrology that are based on biblical readings are assuredly incorrect. Most, if not all, of such pronouncements are rooted in the First, Second, and Third Commandments. We know that the Ten Commandments were given to Moses by God upon making an original covenant with the Hebrew people after their escape from bondage in Egypt. The first three commandments read as follows:

> First Commandment: *"Thou shalt have no other Gods before me"* (Exodus 20:3).

> Second Commandment: *"Thou shalt not make unto thee any graven image, or any likeness of any thing that is in heaven above, or that is in the earth beneath, or that is in the water under the earth"* (Exodus 20:4).

> Third Commandment: *"Thou shalt not bow down thyself to them, nor serve them: for I the Lord thy God am a jealous God"* (Exodus 20:5).

Within this context, the Second and Third Commandments specifically condemn any *worship* of the "graven image." Notice that the New King James version translates these words a little differently. Instead of saying "any graven image," it more specifically states *"a carved image"* (Holy Bible, New King James Version). It is important to realize that the simple act of drawing a map, such as a geological map, an astronomical map, or an astrological horoscope, has no vital meaning of condemnation *unless* it is accompanied by the act of worship.

Anyone reading the Old Testament will become acutely aware that the ancient Hebrews sporadically performed idol worship and pagan idolatry. During the time period that the Hebrew Bible was written, numerous surrounding cultures performed pagan rituals and worshiped the sun, moon, planets, and other pagan gods. Among the Hebrews themselves, the worship of the sun was said to be widespread. One of Josiah's reforms had been to destroy the temple dedicated to the sun because "men worshiping the sun was an abomination" (BiblicalTraining n.d.). As we have seen, such worship clearly violates the Ten Commandments and the Jewish covenant with God. But some of these same passages that were used to instruct the Hebrews in avoiding the practice of idolatry have been erroneously applied as an indictment of astrology. Let us look at a few of these passages more closely.

In Deuteronomy, Moses repeatedly exhorts his people to avoid any kind of practice of idolatry.

> And lest thou lift up thine eyes unto heaven, and when thou seest the sun, and the moon, and the stars, even all the host of heaven, shouldst be driven to worship them, and serve them, which the Lord thy God hath divided unto all nations under the whole heaven (Deuteronomy 4:19).

And again,

> If there be found among you, within any of thy gates which the Lord thy God giveth thee, man or woman, that hath wrought wickedness in the sight of the Lord thy God, in transgressing his covenant, and hath gone and served other gods, and worshiped them, either the sun, or moon, or any of the host of heaven, which I have not commanded; . . . then shalt thou bring forth that man or that woman, which have committed that wicked thing, unto thy gates, even that man or that woman, and shalt stone them with stones, till they die (Deuteronomy 17:2–3, 5).

In an effort to dissuade the Hebrew people from the practice of idolatry, many other examples abound throughout the Old Testament. Passages involve the worship of molten images (2 Kings 17:16); the worship of alters for Baal (2 Kings 21:3–6); the worship of the sun, moon, and all the host of heaven (Jeremiah 8:1–2); or a combination of the worship of Baal and the host of heaven (Zephaniah 1:4–6).

Notice that every one of these exhortations involves the *act of worship*, which most assuredly does not apply to astrology. This distinction is vital. Astrologers act to learn and apply the wisdom of God obtained from their study of God's creation. Absolutely no worship of idols or heavenly bodies occurs in the study of astrology.

You can cite all the passages you want from the Bible, but you will not find even one single passage that exhorts people to avoid the *wisdom or study* of astrology. Quite the contrary, since astrologers were the wise men of old. These individuals were thoroughly and completely sanctioned as being men of God, attaining wisdom and knowledge beyond that of other men, obtaining the richness of God's blessings, and as such were perfectly described in the books of Proverbs, Psalms, Daniel, and elsewhere.

Chapter III
Historical Evidence:
EARLY CHRISTIANITY, ROME, AND THE PAPACY

Over the past 2,000 years, the New Testament has potentially been rewritten, translated, and edited several times. I often speculate on whether some of the ancient language and texts have been changed, and how much original material has been removed or lost. Biblical historians and Palestinian archaeologists continue to discover examples of text and meanings that were modified from the initial gospels attributed to the first apostles. In this respect, one historian confirms: "There was a lot of discussion and debate about it, there were a number of editions of New Testaments. One of the points I must stress: There were a great deal of alternatives offered along the way" (Harl 2001). Particularly over the course of the second century CE, a large number of competing Christian churches evolved, along with their competing testaments.

In a book detailing the life, history, and prophecies of Jesus, Professor James Tabor meticulously examined as much evidence as possible that is available to historians today. Much of his evidence is based on concrete archaeological records and original first-person accounts. Dr. Tabor specifically identifies many areas of later editing and the explicit removal of text that occurred during the first few centuries after the death of Christ, particularly up to or around the fourth century CE (Tabor 2006).

Other biblical scholars investigating early Christian writings verify Dr. Tabor's information. The criterion for the admission of texts into the sacred canon of the New Testament "was not so much that traditions vindicated an apostolic authorship as that the content of the books was in line with the apostolic proclamation received by the second-century churches" (Chadwick 1990). During the year 165 CE, as custodian of the canon, the early Church of Rome clearly played the decisive role in the inclusion, exclusion, and editing of every single word found today in the New Testament. An oral Christian tradition plus many competing books, epistles, and gospels created an impetus for the Church of Rome to define a standard and authoritative version according to their own interpretation. On its official website, the Church of Rome unequivocally states that "the Catholic Church is entirely responsible for the composition of the Bible," and thus one hundred percent of the content was edited and included or excluded according to their intense scrutiny (Catholic Online News Consortium 2014).

Today we understand there were a great many personal accounts of Christ's life, ministry, crucifixion, and death that were passed down orally from disciples and other eyewitnesses to historical events (see Luke 1:1–2). These accounts were variously recorded within about fifty years of Christ's death, generally before the beginning of the second century (Haskins 1993). Yet only a small number were chosen by the Roman church to be included in the New Testament canon.

One Christian scholar precisely asks the following question: "Or did the church actively *create* the canon in response to . . . writings [that were] either more or less than the church accepted?" That scholarly author then provided his own affirmative answer, yes, to this basic question (Chadwick 1990). In other words, several biblical authors have agreed that when the Church of Rome did not explicitly approve of the wording or message found within the original Christian text, then the text was removed or changed accordingly.

The situation is expertly explained here by Princeton University professor of religion Dr. Elaine Pagels: "After the crucifixion, various Christian sects arose, each telling their own story of Jesus from a different point of view. To create a uniform religion, the first church fathers chose four gospels—Matthew, Mark, Luke, and John—which later became the first four books of the new Testament. Dozens of other gospels were declared heretical, and were hidden, lost to history, until discovered in the Egyptian desert in 1945." Dr. Pagels continues by saying that the discovery of the Gnostic gospels "became a treasury" of over fifty writings attributed to Jesus and his disciples. "While the traditional church sought to oversee a person's relationship with God, the Gnostics believed that spiritual revelation could only come from within. No intercession was required by priests or rabbis" (Pagels 2006). For obvious reasons, then, this type of Gnostic thinking was denounced as heretical by the Church of Rome.

THE GNOSTIC GOSPELS

The Gnostic texts were found hidden away within an ancient jar that had been concealed under a boulder in the Egyptian desert near Qumran, around the year 400. Several papyrus books with fifty-two treatises on the life and teachings of Christ survived and are now reassembled and housed in the Coptic Museum in Cairo. Biblical scholars assert that the texts were most likely hidden for safekeeping by monks or believers around 1,600 years ago.

Those texts retrieved in the desert appear to be copies of Greek originals that were initially written in the late first century, soon after the crucifixion occurred. Thus, the Gnostic gospels were written contemporaneously with the other New Testament gospels. They were later reproduced by scribes prior to the year 400, most probably in a monastery, and being considered heretical the texts were hidden to avoid certain destruction by Roman church authorities (Haskins 1993).

Who were the Gnostics, and what did they believe? Fundamentally, the Gnostics were a group of early Christian followers of Christ, many of whom were eyewitnesses, later to become separated from the main dogma of the Church of Rome. Their beliefs became known as *gnosis*, or knowledge derived from spiritual insight. "This *gnosis* was essentially mystical, concerning the nature of God and human existence, and the divine realm of being. . . . The Gnostics' claim to have a superior comprehension of God and their own spiritual nature, together with their claim that this came to them through personal revelation, set them apart from the other Christians, who accepted their beliefs through the mediation of bishops and clergy; for this reason, the orthodox Church regarded them with the utmost suspicion" (Haskins 1993, 32).

Against the growing hierarchy and institutionalization of the Roman church, the Gnostics believed that all individuals were equal under God without regard to sexual discrimination or rank. Through their belief in the individual ability to receive religious revelation, the Gnostics regarded interference from the clerical hierarchy as unwanted and unnecessary. As a result of their theological differences, the Gnostics were declared heretics by the Church of Rome. "Until the nineteenth century, Gnosticism itself and its adherents were only known from the reports written by their orthodox opponents, particularly Irenaeus, Tertullian (*c.* 160–*c.* 225), Origen (*c.* 185–254), Hippolytus of Rome (*fl.* 200), and Epiphanius (*c.* 315–403)," who were all known to describe the Gnostics "with an inevitable bias, in order to refute their beliefs" (Haskins 1993, 32).

Clearly, due to the limited number of Gnostic texts available today, compared to this multitude of theological writings against them, and due to the fact that those texts that are now available were only more recently found deeply hidden in places of concealment, it becomes apparent that the Church of Rome went to enormous lengths to completely destroy any and all of the Gnostic writings.

There is reason to believe that many other texts contrary to the teachings of the Roman church were also deliberately manipulated or destroyed. "According to Eusebius (*c.* 260–*c.* 340), the 'Father of Church History,' it was the policy of the triumphant Church after the pact with Constantine to destroy all the writing of the heretics. It was a policy that Augustine sustained when he advised that all Manchurian writings be burned, having once been an adherent to that sect himself" (Haskins 1993, 54).

IS THE IDEA OF REINCARNATION HERESY?

Another example of the almost utter destruction of writings as a direct result of being declared heretical by the Church of Rome is worth mentioning here. Eminent modern psychiatrist and strong proponent of reincarnation Dr. Brian L. Weiss states that through his close professional work with patients, he is convinced in the reality of reincarnation, despite a complete inability to validate the idea of reincarnation by using the scientific process. Through thousands of working sessions with hundreds of patients undergoing hypnosis therapy, Dr. Weiss discovered an enormous number of patients who clearly described previously forgotten former lives, complete with historical details they could never have known in any other way.

Dr. Weiss is confident that many references to reincarnation were originally found within the writings of the New Testament, only to be purged by the Church of Rome. He goes on to relate information from the Second Council of Constantinople, held in 553 (the same council that is sometimes called the Fifth Ecumenical Council). Not only were those purging actions by the Roman church discussed and approved by the members of the council, but the idea of reincarnation from that time forward was declared heretical (Weiss 1988).

This information can be confirmed elsewhere. "Many scholars believe that the Fifth Ecumenical Council (553 AD) deleted most verses addressing reincarnation from the Bible. But why? The reasons are simple. The church elders wanted the general populace to believe that it was only through the church and its elders could anyone communicate with God or ever hope to reach heaven. This kept all power within the church versus within the people themselves" (McDonald 2011).

Yet today, can we find any references to reincarnation that were not completely purged from the Bible? Some scholars believe that the description of John the Baptist as having returned *"in the spirit and power of Elias"* (Luke 1:17) very clearly demonstrates a belief in reincarnation (Everything Heaven 2016). We hear Jesus repeating the same idea when he, too, refers to John the Baptist as Elias having come again: *"But I say unto you, that Elias is come already, and they knew him not"* (Matthew 17:12).

Indeed, the questions posed by the disciples in yet another passage even more manifestly indicate a belief in reincarnation. When asking Jesus why a man they encountered was born blind, the disciples said, *"Master, who did sin, this man or his parents, that he was born blind?"* (John 9:1–2). Without any doubt, if the man had been *born* blind, there is no way he could have committed any precipitating sin during this lifetime, but only during a previous life!

Consequently, beginning in the second century CE, and in the name of Christianity, we know that the Church of Rome endeavored to impose a common system of theology, education, and ritual over the many scattered communities of believers. By binding them all together into the "one Catholic and apostolic church," they authorized themselves (and only themselves) with the unique ability to edit and discard any and all texts that failed to deliver their own orthodox view. As history progressed, it became expressly forbidden to question papal authority in any manner. Over the next 2,000 years, many more manuscripts were subsequently declared heretical, burned, banned, and destroyed by the Roman church authorities.

THE CHURCH OF ROME VERSUS MARY MAGDALENE

In light of the Gnostic texts, various important scholars have begun to understand the role of the Roman church in denying the appropriate recognition of women, particularly in the treatment of Mary Magdalene. Until as late as 1969, and for at least thirteen centuries, the Roman Catholic Church proclaimed, taught, and reinforced the idea that Mary Magdalene was a harlot or prostitute, notwithstanding any real factual evidence. The New Testament gospels do not say anything at all to this effect. Actually, quite to the contrary, Mary Magdalene is "the first person to hear, touch, see, and smell our Lord risen. . . . She's the first person to communicate the knowledge of the resurrection to the world." This female scholar continues, "I was so angry at what the church had done to women in the name of Christianity, I was stone-cold angry" (Haskins 2006).

The first church authority to officially declare that Mary Magdalene should be considered a prostitute was Pope Gregory the Great. In an intentional and shameful sermon delivered in the year 591, Pope Gregory asserted, without any merit or basis to his statements, that Mary Magdalene was the same person as another woman named Mary who had appeared before Jesus at differing times in the gospels. According to one theological source, "Yet they are clearly different women, and Gregory created the prostitute persona from thin air" (Sooner 2006). During later centuries, when several Catholic theologians attempted to rectify this situation by suggesting that the three Marys were actually separate individuals, they were subsequently rewarded with excommunication from the church (Haskins 1993).

The suppression of the Gnostic gospels by the Church of Rome apparently occurred for the same reason, to deny information the church would rather we did not know. In the Gnostic gospel of Thomas, Mary Magdalene is called a "true disciple" of Jesus. The Gnostic gospel of Mary goes on to portray her as a leader with favored status among followers of Christ, and in the Gnostic gospel of Phillip, she is described as "foremost among the Apostles" (Sooner 2006).

Was this information deliberately repressed because women were considered to be a threat to the male patriarchal system condoned by the Church of Rome? Historically, the church adopted the dominant male patriarchal system practically intact from the imperial Roman society, which had officially endorsed the church. Yet, in direct contrast to the Roman system, "Christ is shown throughout his ministry as positive and egalitarian in his attitude toward women, in having them as friends and followers, talking with them freely, making them recipients of what was later to become Christian dogma, and assigning them roles in parables and stories. . . . Just how radical this approach was can be evinced from the gospels themselves, in the reactions of the Pharisees, and of the male disciples who 'wondered among themselves' when they saw Christ talking to the foreigners and social outcast. . . . The gospels show clearly that Christ regarded his women followers as disciples in their own right" (Haskins 1993, 27–28).

Yet another scholar continues with this same theme: "The men of the formative church said we're going to suppress all women, we're going to lie about it, and we're going to lie about what Jesus said" (Matthews 2006). Consequently, numerous researchers have determined that the early Church of Rome was guilty of deceit, manipulation, and maltreatment in a variety of subject matters. Along the same vein, we shall come to the church's maltreatment of astrology in short order.

Historians have documented that women within the early Gnostic churches performed many of the basic religious functions later assigned solely to men by the Church of Rome. Without regard to sexuality, women within the Gnostic churches were able to teach, preach, baptize, offer Eucharist, and perform many other religious functions (Haskins 1993). Thus, the conditions of male hierarchy, male dominance, and overt sexual discrimination apparently did not exist within the early Gnostic churches.

Unfortunately, this early tradition of sexual equality would only last a few decades following the death of Christ. We know that women such as Phoebe and Junia were recognized by the apostle Paul as leaders, apostles, and missionaries within the fledgling churches (see Romans 16:1–7). Paul wrote his letter to the Romans extolling the role of women during the first century after the death of Christ, around 57 or 58 CE (Holy Bible: Authorized King James Version). Mary Magdalene is clearly one of the women who became an ardent apostle of Christ, before the Church of Rome went on to destroy her reputation.

The first patriarch of the emerging Roman church to insist that women should not be entitled to perform various religious functions within the church was Father Tertullian. Writing toward the end of the second century, Tertullian declared that only males should be allowed to perform the functions that women had previously performed in the Gnostic churches. Within the surrounding hierarchal culture that was predominant in Rome, by his reasoning any woman who performed any of these functions would surely place great shame upon the men of the church (Haskins 1993). Thus, contrary to the teachings of Jesus, the Church of Rome endeavored to thoroughly sanction the practice of male dominance and ultimately eroded and denied any place for women within the church.

What has also become clear is that the Roman church frequently changed positions on a number of religious topics according to the political climate of the times. As related by another noted historian, "Various people entered the Roman Empire, embraced the form of Christianity then being practiced by the imperial family, in other words, what was then official, only to have the imperial family and the church turn to a new form of Christianity, leaving them hanging as heretics" (Noble 2002). As we now turn more closely to the history of Rome and the papacy, the relationship of the Roman church to astrology will soon become increasingly apparent.

ROME AND THE PAPACY

Under the rule of Constantine and beginning in 313 CE, for the first time ever, the Church of Rome was allowed to legally hold and transfer property. Rome went on to become the great seat of power for the new Roman Catholic Church. "Constantine created, in effect, an imperial church. In 325 he summoned the first Ecumenical Council of Nicaea. At that council, the emperor wanted a definition of faith, and it was achieved, the so-called Nicene Creed. . . . All of that would be enforced by the imperial government. It is with Constantine that heresy becomes a really definable sin. . . . The Roman imperial government puts its power behind the imperial church and its definition of dogma, and creates a very, very close alliance between the emperors and the bishops. . . . That position of authority and patronage was the gift of Constantine" (Harl 2001).

According to another biblical scholar, beginning around this time "the Church went down the path of decline with astounding rapidity. Soon the bishops in large cities, who had charge of influential congregations, exalted themselves above those in the less important churches, and began to dictate to them. . . . They called themselves patriarchs (ruling fathers), and exercised a supreme power over other churches. . . . The patriarch of Rome claimed the highest authority in the whole Church, and declared himself the successor of Peter. The name 'patriarch' was changed to 'pope' early in the sixth century" (Houghton 1995, 31–32).

As the new hierarchical leaders in the deteriorating culture of Rome, the church patriarchs clearly inherited all the vices and rampant corruption that had so blatantly taken place during the height of the Roman Empire. Soon thereafter, all important decisions were made only under the explicit approval of Rome. Even as early as the year 440 CE, Leo I, the ruling bishop of Rome, declared that no church and no person had the right to question any decision made by the Church of Rome.

As time moved forward, history now provides numerous examples of the political strife precipitated by the unlimited ambition of the pope for power. In this regard, a noted historian provides the following undisputed evidence: "One pope followed another in rapid succession, some being disposed, others cast into prison, and still others murdered. Pope John XII (955–963) was charged by a Roman Synod [an ecclesiastical council] with almost every crime of which depraved human nature is capable. He was said to have drunk to the devil's health, and to have invoked the help of heathen gods and various demons as he threw dice. All in the synod agreed that he was a monster of inequity. . . . Pope Boniface VII, who put his predecessor to death by strangulation in 974, is described by a synod as a 'papal monster, who in his abject depravity exceeds all mortals.' Now if this was said of popes, what was the condition of the lesser clergy?" (Houghton 1995, 51–53).

Much of the historical evidence indicates that the popes and other leaders of the Roman church often exhibited unbridled ambition and freely took advantage of the depraved state of the Roman culture in which they themselves were immersed. Clearly their behaviors were contrary to the teachings of Jesus Christ, who had so admirably stated: *"If any man desire to be first, the same shall be last of all"* (Mark 9:35). It becomes apparent that many of the popes during this time period did not heed the very words of Jesus and subsequently rejected any notion of servitude. It is therefore not surprising that ongoing conflicts between the pope and other religious and secular leaders in the region continued to frequently erupt.

ROMAN VALUES, HIERARCHY, AND EDUCATION

After Christianity became sanctioned by the Roman emperors, early Christians were legally required to identify themselves and to assimilate the dominant values of the surrounding Roman culture. According to another well-known historian, early Christians "inherited a set of institutions ready-made, conformed to a social and political structure which had developed over a long period, and learned to live with a culture which it had little part in creating" (Markus 1990, 66).

Under Constantine, the Christian religion became a source of prestige, political power, and worldly motives. Great social pressure to conform to the emperor's state religion developed within the ruling classes, and legal penalties were enacted against pagans, heretics, and Jews. In a society of fashionable Christianity, "the religion of the establishment was hard to distinguish from real commitment. . . . Christians identified themselves almost without reservation with the political and social order of the Roman empire" (Markus 1990, 67–70). Consequently, within the emerging Roman society, the ruling upper classes and the aristocracy became the bishops of the new church.

Because of their aristocratic background, individuals leading the church shared the values, culture, and outlook of the Roman nobility. It became obvious to at least one historian that "they don't seem to be living a particularly holy life. Well, they were living the kind of life that people of their class lived." The historian went on to note that as the clergy of the Church of Rome became "increasingly aristocratic," they claimed a prominent role in the government of their regions and obtained enormous prestige from their designated offices, while at the same time, greatly influencing the management of their society (Noble 2002).

Accordingly, church clerical society became notably hierarchical in nature, having the pope in charge directly above the archbishops, who were above the bishops, who were in turn above the priests. While maintaining an autocratic system of hierarchy themselves, they were highly influential in reinforcing a continuation of the same aristocratic ideas of status and rank everywhere within the surrounding culture. Church leaders frequently became key advisors to the empirical rulers. Often, the only schools, libraries, or places of learning were maintained within those same churches and cathedrals. Since the only teachers available to the rest of society came from the Roman church, a long process of continuing aristocratic ideology was clearly maintained without interruption throughout the entire medieval period. This system, of course, was entirely beneficial for the advancement of the clergy, the church patriarchs, and their secular benefactors.

From this point onward, until late in the fifteenth century, nearly all education and books were under the absolute control of the Church of Rome. The reasons were many:

volumes of books were expensive and laboriously written by hand, ink and paper were scarce or nonexistent, and virtually no one except the clergy or nobility knew how to read. The only people who had the ability, the access, or the inclination to write books were the clergy themselves. The printing press was not developed until around 1457, at which time the Gutenberg Bible was printed. Indeed, most books were still being written in Latin, considered the language of the elite. In this matter, the Church of Rome vehemently opposed the use of spoken or native languages during the writing of books, insisting on Latin, which then, unfortunately, led to an even-greater, and apparently deliberate, limitation on the education of the masses (Manchester 1992).

THE PAPAL STATES

During the seventh century CE, the Roman Catholic Church itself became a sovereign state. After the fall of Rome and commensurate with continuing regional conflicts, the pope became the largest landowner in Italy. This immense property ownership, along with the subsequent wealth that this ownership created, brought power. The papacy began to take on much of the ruling authority that the Byzantines were unable to protect around the city of Rome. In practice, the Duchy of Rome became an independent state ruled entirely by the pope (Schnürer 1912).

Rome then became the capitol of the Papal States, the territories on the Italian peninsula under the direct sovereignty of the pope, a rule that dated from the 600s until 1870. The Papal States were considered to be the worldly manifestation of the temporal power of the pope, and through these worldly holdings, the Church of Rome became enormously wealthy.

Given this history, it was natural for the Roman Catholic Church and its dominant Catholic historians to present Constantine as a virtuous and ideal ruler and to shower him with tremendous praise. Yet, other later writers have developed a different perspective of Constantine as a tyrant and scheming secularist. In a newer interpretation presented by more-modern researchers, Constantine is shown to be a plotting politician who was deliberately corrupted by church influences and who then manipulated the circumstances surrounding a pursuit of his own political power. According to this view, Constantine developed an interest in protecting the Church of Rome only after witnessing its pragmatic usefulness in the development of his own political career (Cameron 2005).

Some historians even doubt whether Constantine was a true convert to Christianity. Whatever his motivations, after centuries of persecution and for the first time, the

Roman emperor became a defender of the Christian faith. "But with toleration came danger. It now became an honour and a distinction to be a Christian. The best positions in State and community were given to them. . . . And how the outward appearance of the Church changed! Instead of primitive simplicity came pride and pomp, for the reproach of the cross was turned into royal fame and glory. . . . From this time the Church became a rich 'corporation,' and a worldly spirit entered it. Before long, bishops ruled in large cities as pagan governors had formerly done; they set an example of luxurious living, which contradicted the instruction of the Master, 'Take my yoke upon you and learn of me; or I am meek and lowly of heart.' The greatest danger threatening Christianity was realized when the emperor decided that he himself would rule the Church . . . and such meetings were presided over in his [the emperor Constantine's] name" (Houghton 1995, 20–21).

The Dark Ages:
THE CONTINUING HISTORY OF THE POPES

Beginning with the fall of Rome in 410, Europe quickly fell into the period of time that we now know as the Dark Ages. Many egregious actions of the popes occurred during this time period. Throughout the centuries following the death of Christ, historians have recorded quite a long list of atrocities committed by the patriarchs of the Church of Rome, some of which were duly recorded by the scribes of the Vatican who were adept at keeping diaries.

For instance, in a detailed description of the medieval era, one scholar writes: "At any given moment the most dangerous enemy in Europe was the reigning pope. It seems odd to think of the Holy Fathers in that light, but the five Vicars of Christ who ruled the Holy See during Magellan's lifetime [ca.1480–1521] were the least Christian of men: the least devout, least scrupulous, least compassionate, and among the least chaste—lechers, almost without exception. Ruthless in their pursuit of political power and personal gain, they were medieval despots who used their holy office for blackmail and extortion" (Manchester 1992, 37).

Not only had the popes clearly inherited the legacy of the Roman emperors, they continued to live exactly like their predecessors. "They were the wealthiest men in the world, and they and their cardinals further enriched themselves by selling holy offices." Pontificates were purchased by appointees, much of whose incomes were required to go to Rome. Archbishops paid huge sums for their rank, and all personal possessions were claimed by the church at the time of their death. By decree of the Church of Rome, every single Christian who was living in Europe was subject to papal fees and taxation. The clergy "grew fat and frequently supported concubines on their fees and tithes" (Manchester 1992, 132–133).

By 1502, a financial expert of the times estimated that the Church of Rome owned seventy-five percent of all the land and wealth available in France. At the same time, the church was estimated to own another fifty percent of all the land and wealth available in Germany (Manchester 1992). These holdings were, of course, quite enormous, in addition to those in many other countries.

According to several painstakingly recorded diaries written during the fifteenth and sixteenth centuries, the Roman popes were well known to keep mistresses; promiscuity and orgies at the Vatican became commonplace. Indeed, "the occupants of Saint Peter's chair were openly acknowledging their bantlings, endowing their sons with titles and their daughters with dowries. In the Vatican, nepotism ran amok" (Manchester 1992, 132–133).

Popes proceeded to name their own relatives, such as cousins, illegitimate sons, young nephews, and grandnephews, as archbishops and cardinals, often while they were still children, and even as young as eight years old. At least two of these appointed relatives went on to become popes themselves (Manchester 1992).

While the "winners" in any historical era generally succeed in writing the majority of the history for that particular era, we do know the fate of one idealistic Florentine friar named Girolamo Savonarola (1452–1498). Bravely protesting the papal excesses listed above, Savonarola initiated an annual "bonfire of the vanities" in which he burned items he had removed from the papal palace. These items included gaming tables, extravagant personal ornamentations, lewd pictures, and pornography, all of which had been personally utilized by the popes. For his reward, the Church of Rome condemned him as a heretic, excommunicated him, tortured him, and then hanged him, at which point his body was ultimately and finally burned (Manchester 1992).

Clearly, in every important matter, the pope had *become* the new Roman emperor. The pope's rule over his subjects was absolute; his rule was never questioned for more than a thousand years. As supreme leader of Europe, the pope ordered military actions, waged wars, extracted taxes, and ordered princes, kings, and local leaders to do his bidding. Every sovereign in Europe was bound by law to follow the orders of the pope. Absolutely anyone who dared defy the pope risked excommunication, declaration of heresy, extradition, and, most frequently, an untimely death. All challenges to the pope were, by definition, considered heretical and thus were punishable by death.

Just the sheer fear of excommunication in itself, and its "capacity to inspire absolute terror," gave the papacy a tremendous and overwhelming control over the masses.

After all, the pope had the ability to "determine how each individual would spend his afterlife. . . . His decision might be whimsical, his blessings were often sold openly, his motives might be evil, but that was his prerogative" (Manchester 1992, 42–44).

THE BEGINNING OF THE REFORMATION

Yet, as time moved forward, a smolder of discontent among the faithful eventually began to grow, and reaction against continuing papal excesses would lead to the first act of the religious Reformation. This act was made in response to the sale of indulgences, along with the naked avarice of the papacy who extracted them. Indulgences were payments made to the Church of Rome for the atonements of sins. In other words, the complete remission of guilt could be obtained by paying a monetary fee to the Roman church. The sinner could buy an absolution from sin and therefore become free to sin again. As one historian notes, "the commercialization of indulgences had transformed the Church into a 'money machine'" (Manchester 1992, 92). Indulgences were often sold by the clergy for anything of value, including the services of prostitutes and even carnal indiscretions performed by the supplicants themselves, mainly for the personal benefit and pleasure of the clergy.

The Reformation officially began on October 31, 1517, when Martin Luther, himself a Catholic monk, bravely posted his *Disputation for the Clarification of the Power of Indulgences* on the door of his local church. He then made a copy in German (also against papal policy) and sent another copy to the archbishop in charge of indulgences in the German region. Included were his ninety-five theses, citing objections to the peddling of pardons by the Church of Rome. Astonishingly, "Luther had done the unthinkable—he had flouted the ruler of the universe. . . . In defying the organized Church, Luther had done something else. He had broken the dam of medieval discipline. By his reasoning, every man could be his own priest" (Manchester 1992, 140–143).

During the centuries leading up to Martin Luther, church and state were inextricably intertwined with one another. Then as the printing press began to flourish, books gradually became more available, and fragments of the gospels also began to circulate. Peasants came to see Christ as a supporter of the oppressed rather than as a supporter for their ruthless ecclesiastical rulers. Even the upper classes, who up to that time had shown unwavering support for the clergy, began to question the financial policies of the Church of Rome.

Fortunately, Luther found himself under the protection of a German ruler who did not expressly follow papal orders to extradite him. In 1518, just a few months after the posting of his *Disputation*, German scholars began to pronounce themselves as Lutherans for the very first time; such an amazingly courageous religious movement had never happened before. Luther eventually went on to become the voice for millions of Europeans who, for more than a thousand years, had been mercilessly imprisoned, controlled, impoverished, and afflicted by a lengthy succession of Roman popes (Manchester 1992).

WHY DOES THIS HISTORICAL BACKGROUND MATTER?

In 1517, the audacity of Martin Luther signaled the beginning of a bold new era. But what does the long list of atrocities attributed to the popes mean for us today? How do discussions of the inherited hierarchal role of the Roman church, the history of blatant papal indiscretion, the editing and destruction of texts, the declarations of heresy to subdue theological rivals, and the distortion of the role of women have to do with astrology? Clearly, this background becomes the stage upon which our discussion of astrology is set.

It is positively essential to understand that the entire geopolitical surroundings of the era with which we are concerned remained strictly under the control of, first, the Roman emperors, and next, the Roman popes. When the Roman Empire fell, the absolute control of the emperor was almost universally transferred to the Church of Rome, whose popes ruled for many long centuries following the death of Christ. After the advent of Christianity, and beginning with pervasive edicts emanating from converted Roman emperors, the original writings of the New Testament were placed under the complete and absolute control of the early Church of Rome. Often motivated solely for political purposes, as we shall see, the Church of Rome deplored the teachings of astrology.

How these themes are explicitly related to astrology will be explored in greater depth in a later chapter. But for now, let us say it becomes quite evident that the early Church of Rome had enormous and absolute influence on the writings of the New Testament. That absolute control was initiated by Constantine during the height of the Roman Empire, continued unabatedly into the Middle Ages, and assuredly affects us very deeply yet today. Particularly included was the ominous ability to change, purge, or eliminate as many positive references to astrology as possible within the original scripture of the gospel.

Chapter IV
THE PHILOSOPHICAL
TRADITION OF ASTROLOGY

Before returning to Roman politics and a continued understanding of the era surrounding the birth of Christ, let us look briefly at the background of astrology to gain a greater comprehension of its philosophical tradition. The oldest undisputed written evidence on the use of astrology has been attributed to tablets found in Mesopotamia that were dated around 1651 BCE, but it is possible that other ancient Sumerian texts related to astrology may have been written even before that date (Campion 2008).

We do know that the ancient Babylonians viewed astronomical events as celestial signs emanating from what they considered to be their many higher gods or deities. A parallel but separate concept was developed by the ancient Jews, in that celestial events were viewed as divine signs derived from their one and only higher deity, Yahweh, also known as Jehovah, whom the Jews declared to be their one true Hebrew God.

Early Babylonian astrology holds numerous similarities to the astrology seen later during the Greek Hellenistic period (the time period identified by historians as the three to four centuries just prior to the birth of Christ). Each type of astrology included reference to the circle of the celestial zodiac and used twelve sign divisions, with thirty mathematical degrees per sign (for a total of 360 degrees in the zodiac circle). Also included were the "trine" aspect of 120 degrees, and the planetary exaltations (we will return to many of these concepts in greater detail later on in this book).

The first known written documentation of the astronomical zodiac occurred somewhat earlier than the actual known use of astrology. Distinctive evidence pertaining to the astronomical zodiac was found within a set of Babylonian tablets dated to approximately 2000 BCE. These tablets set out a listing of the stars and constellations that identified the path of the moon through the sky (Campion 2008). This original lunar zodiac contained all of the twelve celestial signs in what we now know as the solar zodiac. At some unknown later date, the lunar zodiac was essentially revised into the solar zodiac. It contained the same twelve zodiac signs, but it differed by following the path of the sun, rather than the path of the moon, as seen from Earth. The twelve-sign solar zodiac is the system still being used today. Due to a belief that the grand celestial design created by God had a divine intent, the symbol of twelve was repeatedly recorded by Moses during the entry of the Jews into the promised land (Campion 2012).

THE SEARCH FOR MEANING

In its broadest sense of the word, astrology, as the study of the stars, is a search for meaning in the heavens above. Astronomical events drawn on a map of the heavens were carefully observed to coincide with corresponding patterns of human events occurring simultaneously here on Earth. The astrological symbols eventually evolved to form unique, multicultural, and archetypal symbols that give deep intrinsic meaning to individuals who have been so instructed in the reading of those symbols.

Early and modern astrologers alike frequently use an expression translated from Latin to mean "as above, so below," which is used to indicate this close correspondence between celestial events and human affairs. Believed to have been originally written by Hermes Trismegistus during the second or third century CE, a more complete translation of this ancient text was done by Sir Isaac Newton. His translation reveals the full astronomical correspondence between astrology and the one true God:

> That which is below is like that which is above, and that which is above is like that which is below to do the miracles of one only thing;
> And as all things have been and arise from one by the mediation of one: so all things have their birth from this one thing by adaptation (Newton, ed., Newman 2010).

Here the words "from this one thing" describe the one true God, whereby all other "things" are made from God, derive from God, and are mediated by God. Obviously, all these other things include the sun, moon, and stars, and any natural correspondences or relationships thereof.

We must remember that a correspondence does not necessarily imply cause. The apparent motions of the planets may be related to events on Earth but do not necessarily cause those events. The principal of acausal synchronicity, which conceptualizes the dramatic coincidence in time between Earth and sky, was developed by psychologist Carl Jung in the mid-twentieth century and was later skillfully addressed by Richard Tarnas (Tarnas 2007). These works bring heightened awareness and modern attention to the not-uncommon experience of correspondence, coincidence, and synchronicity. As contemporary humans continue to search for meaning in life, we return to the synchronicity of Earth and sky, as seen through the lens of astrology.

The following passages from Tarnas may help provide additional clarification:

> Accompanying the more profound occurrences of synchronicity was a dawning intuition, sometimes described as having the character of a spiritual awakening, that the individual was herself or himself not only embedded in a larger ground of meaning and purpose but also in some sense a focus of it. This discovery, often emerging after a sustained period of personal darkness or spiritual crisis, tended to bring with it an opening to new existential potentialities and responsibilities. Both because of this felt personal import and because of its startling metaphysical implications, such a synchronicity contained a certain numinosity, a dynamic spiritual change with transformative consequences for the person experiencing it. In this respect, the phenomenon seemed to function, in religious terms, as something like an intervention of grace. Jung noted that such synchronicities were often kept secret or carefully guarded, to avoid the possibility of ridicule concerning an event possessing such significant personal meaning (Tarnas 2007, 51).

It is likely that this potential for ridicule is keeping many people away from any investigations into the subject of astrology. Scientists and many other individuals are clearly biased against the entire subject and are prone to denouncing astrology without questioning their own internal prejudices. Partly to blame for this tendency, no doubt, is the inability by astrologers to explain in what physical manner astrology actually works. Could there be gravitational forces or magnetic forces between the planets that are very minute and extremely difficult to measure yet are leading to these effects?

Along these lines, research into the activity of sunspots has shown a definitive relationship between periods of increased sunspot activity and major human events. Amazingly, sunspot cycles have been proven to correspond with significant periods of human war and peace. Sunspot activity has also been proven to have an important impact on weather cycles on Earth (Forrest 1993). Yet, we really don't know why this happens, only that it does. No theory on the why of astrology, or even sunspot activity, has been definitively accepted, only that they occur at the same moment in time, in a synchronous manner.

The symbolic connection between two otherwise seemingly unrelated events forms the basis for both the theory of synchronicity and astrology as we know it today. According to Tarnas, it was in this manner through meaningful synchronicity that Jung discovered that larger patterns of meaning could be recognized as part of a universal and sublimely ordered whole. However, these new patterns of meaning will necessarily create a challenge for any person's usual or conventional method of conscious thought. An individual must become open to the radical change in thought patterns that are created by the experience of synchronicity.

A PURPOSEFUL INTELLIGENCE

In order to accept astrology, as well as the underlying principle of meaningful correspondence, one must accept a deeper understanding that there is a purposeful intelligence that created the world. Christians will view that creative intelligence as God. Astrologers must also view the heavens above and the entire universe as an intelligently ordered, purposefully designed, and inherently complex development of astronomical correspondence with human life. The planetary movements do not "make" something happen at all, but they do function *along with* corresponding events or activities on Earth. For humans, the planetary movements work as celestial signs, "as above, so below."

Two of the most famous Greek philosophers, Plato and his student, Aristotle, wrote that the universe was essentially purposeful. Born around 428 BCE, Plato developed many ideas that are formative to astrological thought even today. Through his writings, Plato outlined that the creation and structure of the universe and man's place in the cosmos were ordained by God. Plato identified the planets and stars as the principal means for the creator to reveal meaning to humanity. As Campion notes, "For Plato, the order of the heavens was a mirror of divine reason" (Campion 2008, 151).

The writings of Plato also formed the basis for much theological thought over the ages. Plato believed that the soul's primary purpose was to ascend through the heavens in a return to God, and for this purpose, the path of the soul lay through the planetary spheres. Plato believed that nature and the entire universe are controlled by reason, or *logos*, which is itself controlled by God. Consequently, according to Plato, everything that happens in the world does so in accordance with, and as a result of, divine reason (Campion 2008).

To this end and through the study of astrology, the planets and signs can be used to describe a person's life and function as part of a rational, natural philosophy that respects the will of God and endorses a meaningful relationship between humanity, nature, and celestial phenomena. This natural philosophical approach does not reject empirical scientific knowledge in itself at all, but it does reject any explicit or implicit idea of a cold and meaningless universe.

In antithesis to astrology, however, an ultramodern yet unfortunate philosophical view endorsing a meaningless universe is frequently employed or implied by modern scientists, who callously reject astrology without providing any proof against it whatsoever. Science is supposed to include a systematic set of observations and experimentation before any final conclusions can be drawn. Yet, most, if not all, of the individuals rejecting astrology have never studied astrology, know absolutely nothing about it, and do not even respect the basic and fundamental existence of God.

In this regard, Campion points out that the underlying Platonic principles, in which science originally included a profound basis in God, were a philosophy that prevailed in science up through the time of Isaac Newton, and thus, until fairly recently. "It is, in fact, the very conception of modern science that was precious to Newton and prevailed until atheism gained the upper hand in scientific circles in the late nineteenth century. And because each human was the microcosm, an exact mold of the universe, the grand spiritual scheme could be applied to anyone's life" (Campion 2008, 192).

I believe one can truly understand astrology in light of a creative higher intelligence. The profound correspondence between alignments of the celestial bodies with human and mundane activities is overwhelming evidence of an ordered and purposeful universe. Synchronicity means that events are occurring at a simultaneous moment in time. If simultaneous occurrences were to happen only rarely or even occasionally, then they might be seen merely as random events. But when simultaneous occurrences repeat in meaningful patterns that happen over and over again throughout the course of human history, then they can no longer be viewed as random.

Now that we have this important philosophical background freshly in mind, we can continue to investigate certain events taking place within the course of history closely surrounding early Christianity.

Chapter V
AUGUSTINE, POLITICS, AND THE ROMAN CHURCH

So far, we have examined the lengthy tradition of astrology that is increasingly evident within the Old Testament. From its inception, and for at least 2,000 years prior to the birth of Christ, astrology was acknowledged by the Hebrew people to be tightly aligned with both science and Jewish monotheistic religious practice. Celestial astronomy was viewed as a pure reflection of God's will, and the consistent and concurrent manifestation of God's will was reflected in human activity here on Earth. To the ancient Hebrews, astrology became a path leading toward a deeper wisdom and a fundamental understanding of God. This concept is clearly compatible with modern Christianity as we know it today.

We learned how the Church of Rome adopted the Roman hierarchal system and other prevailing cultural factors that had developed over five centuries of Roman rule. Immediately following the fall of the Roman Empire, the church found itself in a prominent position that allowed the complete takeover of state affairs. In so doing, the Church of Rome inherited a patriarchal system denying a role for women, and disinheriting every other system of belief that did not exactly coincide with its own. As such, we found that the Gnostic texts and other early Christian doctrines were declared heretical. Along with the declaration of heresy came threats of death and the nearly complete destruction of all competing texts. Due to the enormous wealth, virtually unlimited power, and absolute fear that were generated by the Church of Rome, all competing systems were subsequently denied a place in Christian belief for over a thousand years.

Astrology became one of those doctrines rejected by the Roman church. Let us therefore examine in more specific detail the reasons for this rejection and the manner in which it occurred. To do so, we must turn to a study of one highly influential bishop within the Church of Rome, a man who is known to the world today as St. Augustine.

First of all, St. Augustine made a very large and quintessential error. Perhaps the error was produced deliberately for political purposes. Nonetheless, Augustine clearly made an erroneous assumption that every type of astrology was a form of *worship* of multiple deities named after the planets (a type of polytheism that continued to be practiced within small pockets in Rome, as well as previously during the Babylonian era). St. Augustine thus misapplied the pagan Roman and Babylonian polytheistic religious dogma to all forms of astrology, including the strictly monotheistic Hebrew astrology. From this point onward, St. Augustine and other patriarchs of the Church of Rome incorrectly stated that any form of astrology conflicted with the basic Christian tenant regarding belief in one true God.

However untrue and unrealistic this accusation may have been, it was from this point onward that the Roman church intentionally began to fight stridently against astrology. Interestingly, the effort led by the church to reject astrology exactly coincided with the prevention of individual access to Christian belief except directly through the Roman priesthood.

It is important to understand the political and cultural context of the era in which these events transpired. During the time of St. Augustine, the Roman Empire had already reached its height and had begun to unravel in its eventual and final decline. Historically, the Roman Empire began in 27 BCE and ended in 476 CE, a period lasting greater than 500 years. Reasons for the fall of the Roman Empire are still being debated today (Alchin n.d.a, n.d.b). However, we know the following facts that are summarized below.

THE ROMAN ARMY

The Romans created a highly organized and unparalleled army of enormous strength, size, and destructive power. During the height of the Roman Empire, their sheer numbers and undisputed military skill virtually overwhelmed any territory that Roman authorities chose to enter. For instance, just in Asia Minor alone, the Roman armies literally took "hundreds of thousands" of slaves, and frequently entire families, villages, and towns were physically forced into slavery. Here the Roman Empire is astutely described by popular historian and professor Kenneth W. Harl, PhD, who in a series of lectures stated:

This Mediterranean empire, which by all standards is probably the most successful of all the ancient empires, at least in the western tradition, and at the time of Augustus, perhaps anywhere from twenty percent to twenty-five percent of humanity were subjects of Augustus the Roman emperor (Harl 2001).

Dr. Harl continues:

In the case of Roman conquest, these wars were far more brutal. . . . Roman armies marched into Greece and Asia Minor, and shocked the locals with what they could do. For one thing, the Romans could take cities with siege craft, and did, trashing them. . . . And really, the Romans, when they went through a city, they took everything, and they enslaved whole populations, reports of 50,000 and 60,000 slaves [from any one city or region]. Probably something in the order of a million people were removed from their homes in the Mediterranean, many of them in the Greek world, and ended up on the Roman slave markets in the late second and first century BC (Harl 2001).

A BRUTAL ROMAN CULTURE

The cruelty of the Roman victors toward their defenseless captives was so completely and overwhelmingly brutal, it is very difficult for us to imagine it today. As an example, during the Jewish uprising in Jerusalem around 70 CE, historians document that as many as 500 Jews were captured and crucified *every single day* by the Romans, in order to terrorize the remaining population of Jerusalem. It has been documented that all the surrounding land around Jerusalem had been stripped clean of trees in order to make crosses for this single purpose. During the first century CE, historian Josephus provided an eyewitness account that described the horror of the Roman crucifixion as the "most wretched of deaths." When hanged on the cross, victims were pierced with nails and were deliberately forced to die a particularly slow and agonizing death. It was a common sight for bodies to be left on the hundreds of crosses surrounding Jerusalem for many days at a time, as death arrived excruciatingly slowly (Tabor 2006).

Meanwhile, political corruption was rampant in Rome, and civil war often thrust the entire empire into chaos. During the second and third centuries CE, more than twenty different rulers had taken the throne as emperors of Rome within a time span of only seventy-five years, usually following the murder of the previous emperor. The Praetorian Guard, who were known as the elite personal bodyguards of the emperor, usually decided who should be disposed and who should become the newest emperor, often on the basis of the highest bidder. An emperor was assassinated and a new one was installed almost at will. Indeed, the emperors themselves were frequently corrupt, incompetent, and excessive (Andrews 2014).

Moreover, the entire Roman Empire was dependent on slave labor. Slaves were captured wherever Roman conquests occurred, and cheap slave labor, in turn, led to high unemployment of the people of Rome. As a result of this practice, a massive divide developed between rich and poor. Gold became the primary motivating factor, and a serious decline in morals rapidly spread. All classes of people were affected by this moral decline, and civil unrest frequently occurred.

Entertainment for the unemployed Romans, who were known as the "mob," became essential to avoid extreme civil violence, and the Coliseum gladiatorial games were sponsored by corrupt politicians in order to placate the Roman people. Along with bloody chariot races and brutal gladiator combats, there is documented evidence to indicate that promiscuity, bestiality, lewd and sexually explicit acts, severe cruelty, and highly sadistic behaviors regularly occurred within the walls of the Roman arena. Innocent victims were often torn apart by dogs, eaten by wild beasts, and set on fire simply for the entertainment of the populace (Alchin n.d.a, n.d.b).

One highly explicit and historically accurate documentary film on the subject matter gives the following detailed information:

> The people who crowded into the Coliseum were drawn there by their lust for blood which flowed in the arena. . . . What is certain is that the crowds never tired of the violence and cruelty on show for their pleasure, resulting in the atrocious deaths of thousands. . . . There was no military victory, religious festival, or anniversary which was not celebrated with bloody combat. In just one of these celebrations, lasting for 117 consecutive days, more than 9,000 gladiators died in the arena (Zappala 1994).

Another historically accurate documentary film goes on to describe various scenes of torture as the Roman emperors of that era decided "to appease the proletariats desire for entertainment by turning the torturing of Christians into a public spectacle. . . . Each night, the followers of Christ were covered with pitch and turned into human torches in order to illuminate the circus performances." It is not possible for us to easily imagine this type of cruelty today. Yet, the film provides many historically accurate details on the brutal and merciless methods that Roman citizens devised to torture Christians and other hapless victims. Various examples included stabbing their victims with forks of hot iron, boiling them in lead, roasting captives on burning grills, and cutting off their hands and tongues. The film then simply asks: "What motivated the Romans to torture them so mercilessly?" (Marcarelli 1991).

We can only merely guess at their final motivations. But as we review this lengthy list of cruel and insidious behavior today, we must remember that the entire Roman population essentially stood behind and repeatedly acted within this merciless, brutal culture. The emperors themselves may have initiated much of the behavior, but the entire Roman citizenry obviously supported, enjoyed, and celebrated that behavior. Thus, the gladiatorial games were observed to become "a definitively Roman institution; that is, the mass slaughter of animals and humans, to show that the Romans are masters of the universe" (Harl 2001).

As the above examples so starkly illustrate, most Roman citizens must have been notoriously and completely indifferent to human suffering in virtually everything they did and everywhere they went. Just to give some idea of the massive size of the Roman Coliseum, it is interesting to note that it could hold three tiers of seating and at least 45,000 spectators, and it was often full to capacity. We know that in the first three centuries after the birth of Christ, a huge number of unfortunate Jews and early Christians were condemned to death and martyred by the Romans. While it is impossible to really know the total number of victims, we do know that public exhibitions of various kinds occurred in the arena almost daily (Houghton 1995).

THE ROLE OF ASTROLOGY

Within this historical context, incoming emperors used astrologers as political pawns to assist in their claims to sovereignty and divine rule. Ever since the existence of the first Roman emperor, all Roman emperors were viewed as the *pontifex maximus*, or the chief priest with sole access to the authority of the Roman gods. Astrologers were periodically banished and then readmitted to the empire as needed to identify and select new emperors, and to identify and kill off their political rivals.

Ultimately, the new emperor required divine verification from celestial omens in order to assure his imperial acceptance. Consequently, astrological omens were periodically manipulated for this purpose. Frequently on the risk of death, astrologers were required to produce the appropriate celestial omens necessary for an emperor's divine verification.

Once in place, as *pontifex maximus*, often a new emperor's first action "was, like his predecessors, to banish the astrologers. The reason was clear. It was not that the astrologers were disreputable or despised or merely foreign: They were too powerful

... that is, in a nutshell, the pagan origin of the doctrine of papal infallibility, inherited by the bishops of Rome, when they usurped the power of the emperor from the fifth century onwards" (Campion 2008, 241). Clearly, the newly installed popes would also go on to adopt a similar attitude toward astrologers, a topic that will be discussed shortly.

Many Roman emperors continued the policy of murdering political rivals whose horoscopes showed the potential to become imperial leaders. Apparently, the murder of political rivals became fairly commonplace during the history of the Roman Empire. Here we are reminded of the famous scene in *The Tragedy of Julius Caesar*, a play written by William Shakespeare describing life just before the initiation of the Roman Empire. In act 1, scene 2, when speaking to Julius Caesar, the soothsayer warns, "Beware the Ides of March," which then became the date on which Caesar was brutally assassinated by his rival Roman senators (Shakespeare, *Julius Caesar*, found online 2015).

Within the rampant corruption of Roman rule, then, astrologers were forced to aid and assist an emperor when necessity demanded, and were themselves killed or discarded when it became politically expedient. As Campion writes:

> The emperors' use of astrology together with fears that it might be used against them, continued throughout the rest of the imperial period down to Constantine and Christianity's final entry into the political arena, after it [Christianity] was legalized in 313. At that point, the two messianic strands in Roman culture, imperial and Christian, came together (Campion 2008, 242–243).

Until 313, the previous Roman emperors had demanded that all subjects of the Roman Empire worship the pagan idols or gods. But at this point, when the conversion of the new Roman emperor Constantine to Christianity occurred, Christianity then became the official state religion of the empire. Under Constantine, and taking advantage of the Roman hierarchal system already in place, the new Roman Christian church was officially sanctioned and began to develop exponentially.

By the year 321 CE, Constantine issued a pervasive edict ordering that all magi and astrologers be put to death. Some astrological practitioners were tortured and burned at the stake. Under the threat of physical violence and extermination by the emperor and his collusive Roman church leaders, for many years astrologers and the study of astrology had no choice but to go underground or to periodically disappear from existence throughout much of the Western world (Jacobi 1907).

Nevertheless, during the decades following Constantine's death, succeeding Roman emperors would intermittently resurrect and benefit from the assistance of astrology. The last decades of the Roman Empire were filled with turmoil, political assassinations, and a frequent change of emperors. Depending on which emperor was involved at the time, the political use of astrology continued to be used as a tool by many imperial leaders, occasionally even including some of the early leaders of the Church of Rome.

ST. AUGUSTINE AND THE
FUTURE OF ASTROLOGY

As we have seen, the conversion of Constantine came with mixed blessings. St. Augustine was born around this time frame during the late Roman Empire, and we must remember the ongoing cultural context of assassination, cruelty, moral depravity, and deep political corruption that was rampant surrounding the entire historical period. It has been documented that the bloody persecution of Christians, as described earlier, began during the first century CE and continued unabatedly for more than three long centuries, up until the conversion of Constantine (Marcarelli 1991).

Countless Roman atrocities were also committed against Jews and other innocent victims. These atrocities had been occurring for a considerable length of time even before the Christians came on the scene. Needless to say, this long period of time hardly represents just a short-term mass psychology but clearly defines the entire Roman culture of that era.

Who was St. Augustine? Born into a prominent Roman family in 354 CE, after the edicts of Constantine had become effective, he was originally named Aurelius Augustinus within the Latin heritage. As a Roman citizen, St. Augustine was surrounded by the brutal political environment of the crumbling Roman Empire. Around the year 396, he was named bishop of Hippo Regius, an important region of the Roman Empire that was located in northern Africa, in what is now Algeria (Portalié 1907).

The time period embracing St. Augustine's life described a vicious climate of sheer political expediency. In spite of Constantine's edicts, we know that astrologers were periodically exiled, forced to return, and subjected to control and manipulation by emperors and other power figures. For purposes of promoting their own personal gain, Roman imperial authorities preferred to have full control over astrologers and the use of astrology, thereby turning astrologers into pawns for their ongoing political power games.

Ongoing civil war between rival generals and the perpetual pressure of barbarian invasion created a recurring imperial crisis surrounding the life of St. Augustine. As emperor, Constantine had transformed the Church of Rome into a state-mandated religion. But it should be noted that many smaller, competing Christian churches and continuing pagan practices still existed within the environment of the declining Roman order. Periodic shifts in the philosophy of the Roman imperial church occurred, and with each change came the denunciation of heresy for any competing religion or ideology. Even old philosophies that the Roman church itself had previously endorsed were later deemed heretical. Amid the turmoil, many small churches and ideologies persisted in serving as rivals and serious political opponents during the final chaotic days of the weakening empire. Here a noted historian describes events in Rome during this remarkable period: "It was an extraordinary scene; there's probably never been a time like it for competing religions, for a ferment of religious activity" (Hale 2009).

It was during this critical period that the breakdown of the prevailing political and social order became increasingly desperate, and the situation commanded St. Augustine's immediate support. The majority of his writings appear to have been used as an instrument to denounce rival churches and ideologies and to support his own state-mandated religion, along with the imperial political order. The denunciation of astrology apparently occupied only a small portion of space in his treatises. Nonetheless, his writings on astrology had far-reaching consequences. St. Augustine wrote his most important works around the years 397 and 410 CE. It was during the same year, in 410 CE, that barbarians invaded and sacked the city of Rome; the extreme urgency and political necessity of his writings thus becomes readily apparent (Campion 2008).

During all the previous centuries encompassing the Roman Empire, the city of Rome had never before been successfully attacked. Success by invaders before 410 would have been completely unimaginable; the bloody defeat left the surviving Romans in a state of shock. Many Romans saw the defeat as punishment from the pagan gods for abandoning their traditional Roman religion and replacing it with Christianity. St. Augustine clearly wrote *The City of God* in response to these accusations, and in order to console his fellow Christians. In so doing, Augustine argued for the truth of Christianity over these other competing religions and philosophies (Encyclopedia Britannica n.d.).

It was in this work that St. Augustine condemned astrology. Campion states that for the future of astrology, "Augustine was judge, jury and executioner. . . . There was no more a single astrology in the fourth century than there was a single Christianity, but Augustine had to pretend there was; otherwise there would be nothing to attack. . . . It is clear that his knowledge of astrology was not great, in spite of his background, and his experience was far more with an astrology of an overtly religious planet-worshiping nature" (Campion 2008, 282). The planet-worshiping or pagan type of astrology to which Campion refers was the ancient type of Babylonian astrology that practiced idolatry and worship of a very large number of deities, gods, and goddesses named after the planets. Evidently, St. Augustine specifically rejected the practice of a multiple-deity Babylonian religion, a type of religion that included idolatry and was therefore not compatible with Christianity.

Other historical writers concur in confirming St. Augustine's lack of detailed or adequate knowledge in the subject of astrology. While at times St. Augustine does seem to demonstrate some knowledge of astrology, one writer states, "It is doubtful whether Augustine ever really did understand the principles of the horoscope" (van der Meer 1961, 61). Another historian writes:

> Augustine's picture of astrology contains some significant inaccuracies. The view of astrology which Augustine presents assumes . . . an absolute fatalism in which every event of a person's life was believed to be completely determined by the horoscope. However, such all-embracing fatalism—though frequently assumed among Christian authors dealing with astrology—was not necessarily held by ancient astrologers themselves. . . . Augustine's presentation of astrology ignores significant distinctions within ancient astrology (Hegedus 2007, 57).

It must be emphasized that the type of multiple-deity pagan astrology rejected by St. Augustine is obviously *not* the same type as the monotheistic Jewish astrology practiced by the ancient Hebrews. As described extensively within the Hebrew Bible, the Jewish astrology that was used and practiced by Abraham and Moses unquestionably proclaims the one true Hebrew God and clearly follows the grand celestial design created by God. Our modern astrology today continues in the same Jewish tradition of the one true supreme creator and does not in any manner follow the religious multiple-idolatry that was practiced by the ancient Babylonians. Neither does modern astrology practice any worship of the planets whatsoever.

The politically motivated denunciations by St. Augustine therefore do not apply to modern astrology, nor does the horoscope reveal or predict a person's supposed destiny or fate. While basic patterns of meaning do emerge from the horoscope, it is entirely up to each person to fulfill his or her own deeper potential and genuine individuality. An individual may apply the astrological patterns and meaning found within the horoscope into his own private life, but that person always acts in accordance with his own basic character, free will, and personal belief in God. As such, the comprehension of planetary movements and astrological patterns never forces or requires a person to do anything but can be used by the individual to assist in a greater personal understanding of God's divine will.

It could not be overemphasized how important the official proclamations of the Church of Rome, which were based on the erroneous political denunciations by St. Augustine, affected the future of astrology. Over the centuries, the Roman Catholic Church has continued to promote the same erroneous policies regarding astrology, up until the present day. Historians have determined that the influence of St. Augustine upon Christianity "would be greater than that of any other man except the apostle Paul," whether upon astrology or any other matters adjudicated by the Church of Rome (Manchester 1992, 9–10). Just to provide one additional example of the enormity of St. Augustine's influence, he became the first church leader to advocate that sex was evil, thus creating another undeservedly harsh Roman church doctrine that has been carried right on down into the twenty-first century.

Clearly, the traditional Hebrew and biblical worldview before the time of St. Augustine recognized that planetary movements within the zodiac signs were guided by the heavens and identified God's will. In our review of significant sections of the Old Testament, we found that the study of astrology provided important knowledge that became part of God's plan for human beings here on Earth. That biblical worldview incorporated a sense of wholeness between heaven and Earth, between the divine and the secular, and between God and human. But the political theology developed by St. Augustine eventually worked to eliminate that original worldview. The next chapter will explore these developments a bit further and will explain how they affected the overall future of astrology.

Chapter VI

THE MODERN WORLDVIEW

The prevailing political atmosphere and overwhelming social influence enjoyed by the Roman Catholic Church during the Middle Ages and throughout the Inquisition continued to assist in their efforts to deny and denunciate astrology. For a great many centuries in the Western world, if it was to survive at all, it was necessary for astrology to go completely underground. Meanwhile, astrology thrived in other parts of the world. Particularly important were astrological studies and texts written in parts of Arabia, from which much of our current knowledge in Western astrology evolved.

As time moved forward, there were several important historical influences that began the process of changing the entire way in which man tended to look at the world. These influences included the eventual adoption of Copernican thinking and, later on, the scientific revolution. Contrary to earlier scientific teachings, the Earth was discovered to actually revolve around the sun. This was revolutionary thinking for the times.

It is interesting to note that the Roman Catholic Church originally condemned the Copernican theory in 1616 and later subjected Galileo to trial by inquisition in 1633 for his part in the development of the heliocentric model (where the sun is placed in the center of the solar system). It is also noteworthy that the theory of heliocentricity is now completely taken for granted by modern civilization.

The importance of these fundamental changes in our worldview is enormous. As Richard Tarnas writes:

> Our world view is not simply the way we look at the world. It reaches inward to
> constitute our innermost being, and outward to constitute the world. It mirrors
> but also reinforces and even forges the structures, armorings, and possibilities
> of our interior life. It deeply configures our psychic and somatic experience, the

patterns of our sensing, knowing, and interacting with the world . . . shaping and working the world's malleable potentials in a thousand ways of subtly reciprocal interaction. World views create worlds (Tarnas 2007, 16).

Tarnas goes on to explain the differences and ramifications between what he defines as the "primal" worldview and the modern worldview. The all-inclusive primal (or natural) worldview was held universally during early biblical times. It was further described and developed by Plato and directly coincides with writings and attitudes depicted in the Old Testament.

In the primal worldview, the individual human self and all of the natural world are part of one great unit or matrix. Changes in one part of the matrix directly affect other parts of the whole. In like manner, a larger purpose and meaning can literally be derived from the signs, placements, and movements of the planetary bodies. Clearly, this was the systematic worldview that was recognized by the ancient Hebrew peoples of the Bible.

In contrast, the modern worldview incorporates a fundamental separation or divorce between the viewer and the objects of his viewing, thereby marking a sharp division between the self and the world around him. Subsequently, people viewing the heavens with a modern worldview see only a huge empty space, a solar system based simply on gravitational principles alone, mechanical-type planetary movements, and a cosmos without intrinsic meaning. In this regard, both in the inception and practice of its basic philosophy, the modern worldview is akin to atheism.

CONSEQUENCES OF THE MODERN WORLDVIEW

There are many profound and unfortunate ramifications that have occurred with the advent of the modern worldview. Inevitably, we take our worldview so much for granted, we hardly realize how deeply it affects us. Our way of looking at the world was created relatively recently by the prevailing scientific philosophy and culture, a system that identifies and emphasizes the stark division between oneself and the rest of the world. Ultimately, this philosophy commonly leads to any of the following serious human contingencies: discordant feelings of separation and alienation, severe personal dissatisfaction, and an increased level of personal anxiety and disenfranchisement.

These conditions always seem to worsen when humans are forced to live in crowded, concrete, urban environments, where nature and natural areas are increasingly difficult to find and personally experience. The radical shift to the modern worldview actually necessitates a deep chasm between human beings and the rest of the natural world. We no longer participate in the world around us in the same manner. We have become observers of nature rather than participants.

Consequently, individuals become increasingly disempowered, disaffected, and totally differentiated from their natural surroundings. As separate entities, what we do to the world in terms of pollution, criminal activities, and the destruction of other human beings does not seem to affect us personally. The resultant list of human crises includes global terrorism, worldwide environmental degradation, rampant gang activity, plutocracy by the wealthy, and severe government despotism, all of which are not seen to be our own personal problems.

The modern differentiation between oneself, the world, and God was unknown during the early Hebrew tradition as seen in the Old Testament. As an intrinsic part of this tradition, astrology continued for perhaps three centuries after the death of Christ and into the beginnings of early Christianity. But in the era surrounding Constantine, as we have seen, overwhelming political strife led to denunciations of astrology by the victorious Roman church. The continuing threats, tortures, suffering, and deaths engendered by the powerful Church of Rome against astrologers forcefully annihilated nearly all Western allegiance to astrology.

The radical change from the primal worldview to the modern worldview helped seal the demise of astrology. People in the Western world were given no choice but to comply, or they would be forced to endure constant harassment, ridicule, and often the menace of death. These threats of ridicule and harassment are still happening today.

THE WORLDVIEW OF ASTROLOGY

Astrology, with its fundamental concepts of wholeness, unity with God, and correspondence between human activities and the planets, stars, and celestial bodies, is a systematic thought process that embraces the principles of the natural or primal worldview. The advent of the modern worldview, together with the commanding influence of the Roman Catholic Church, created enormous cultural conditions affecting astrology. Western astrology was compelled to disappear, along with its corresponding worldview, a view so freely evident within the Old Testament.

During the intervening centuries, some variations of astrology did occasionally resurface in the Western world. Most notably, William Lilly's *Christian Astrology* was initially published in 1647 in London, England. Considered as one of the greatest astrologers of all time, Lilly incorporated methods that are still being studied today, and most fortunately, his volumes are now being republished. Coming shortly after the Inquisition, it is instructive to read Lilly's words. Using the old English language and spelling, Lilly states the following:

> Sir, I hope you shall have no dishonor to Patronize the Ensuing Worke, wherein I lay downe the whol natural grounds of the Art, in a fit Method: that thereby I may undeceive those, who misled by some Pedling Divines, have upon no better credit than their bare words, conceived Astrology to conflict upon Diabolicall Principles: a most scandalous untruth, foysted into both the Nobility and Gentries apprehensions, to deter them from this Study, and to reserve it intyre unto their owne selves (Lilly 2004, ix–x; first published in 1647).

The eventual and gradual rebirth of astrology over the past century has not been without its detractors. Yet, the principles of astrology remain untarnished, in spite of the fact that, as Lilly so aptly writes, those detractors have used "no better credit than their bare words." Described here by Lilly as "Divines," the astrological detractors in his time appear to be cut from the same political cloth as those from an earlier time period, and thus similarly authorized by the Church of Rome.

Within the modern era, many of the people who denigrate astrology most harshly have neither studied nor bothered to actually learn anything about the subject. True science involves a logical investigation, the examination of evidence, empirical observation, structured experimentation, and ordered thinking. When the rare true scientific investigation is performed by detractors of astrology, their conclusions are forced to change.

To this end, Richard Tarnas writes about an extensive examination by a prominent academic psychologist who was unsympathetic to astrology back in 1982. In a publication reporting the conclusions of the investigation, Hans Eysenck and David Nias concluded:

> We feel obliged to admit that there is something here that requires explanation. However much it may go against the grain, other scientists who take the trouble to examine the evidence may eventually be forced to a similar conclusion. The findings are inexplicable but they are also factual, and as such can no longer be ignored; they cannot just be wished away because they are unpalatable or not in accord with the laws of present-day science (Eysenck and Nias 1982).

Thus, it appears that persons who actually become involved in a true scientific investigation of astrology would become convinced of astrology's veracity. Certainly, in order to perform this type of research, one must literally "go against the grain" and throw off the blinders imposed by society's prevailing worldview.

UNDERSTANDING THE BIRTH CHART

Tarnas goes on to state that an understanding of the basic dynamic nature of the birth chart

> allows one to bring greater awareness to the task of fulfilling one's authentic nature and intrinsic potential. . . . This is the basic rationale for depth psychology, from Freud and Jung onward: to release oneself from the bondage of blind action and unconsciously motivated experience, to recognize and explore the deeper forces in the human psyche and thereby modulate and transform them. On the individual level, astrology is valued for its capacity to articulate which archetypes are especially important for each person, how they interact with each other, and when they are most likely to be activated in the course of each life (Tarnas 2007, 78).

Individuals must take full responsibility for their own actions, successes, and failures throughout life. While the birth chart can show certain individual talents, potentials, and tendencies, each person is inherently unique and must develop himself independently. The birth chart can work like a map that allows you to develop your own potential with greater ease of navigation. If you know where the road ahead is blocked, then you can choose to temporarily go in another direction in order to reach your eventual final destination.

Astrology essentially helps us to understand more profoundly about the grand unity of the cosmos. On the earthly plane, we are required to develop our own personal set of beliefs and moral codes that govern our actions, individual relationships, and interactions with other people. The more deeply we learn about astrology, the more apparent it all becomes that there is a fundamental interdependence of individual parts within the whole. Within the process of our personal development, we become more attuned to the presence and nature of God.

Over the next few pages, we will demonstrate this process of understanding as we delve into the historical background, astrological horoscope, and enduring legacy of the key biblical figure and Hebrew ruler known as King David.

Chapter VII
THE ASTROLOGY OF SAMUEL AND DAVID

The story of Samuel and David is an integral part of Jewish history and the Old Testament that reverberates yet today. A closer review of the background of this story can help us understand some of the meaningful uses of astrology, and how astrology may have been employed during ancient biblical times. First, let us set the scene with some information on Samuel. During the time before David was born, when Samuel was yet very young, it was told:

> And the Lord came, and stood, and called as at other times, Samuel, Samuel.
> Then Samuel answered, Speak; for thy servant heareth. . . . Samuel grew, and the
> Lord was with him, and did let none of his words fall to the ground. And all Israel
> from Dan even to Beer-sheba knew that Samuel was established to be a prophet
> of the Lord (I Samuel 3:10, 19–20).

We know that historically, Samuel was prophet and counselor before and during the time of King Saul. However, in the second year of his reign, Saul was said to have disobeyed God, and since he *"hast not kept the commandment of the Lord"* (I Samuel 13:13), Samuel was then dispatched by the Lord to find a new king for Israel:

> And the Lord said unto Samuel, How long wilt thou morn for Saul, seeing I
> have rejected him from reigning over Israel? Fill thine horn with oil, and go, I
> will send thee to Jesse the Bethlehemite, for I have provided me a king among
> his sons (I Samuel 16:1).

Then did Samuel go find Jesse, who brought before Samuel seven of his sons to pass before him. But Samuel did not choose any of them, saying, *"The Lord hath not chosen these"* (I Samuel 16:10). Samuel then requested Jesse to fetch his youngest son, David, who was away tending the sheep. This action was clearly unprecedented during biblical times. Especially with so many available sons before him, it was extremely unusual that Samuel would have overlooked the older sons in favor of choosing the very youngest son!

Here the text is not very specific about how Samuel knew that David was to become the chosen king, except to give Samuel the following instructions:

> But the Lord said unto Samuel, Look not on his countenance, or on the height of his stature; because I have refused him: for the Lord seeth not as man seeth; for man looketh on the outward appearance, but the Lord looketh on the heart (I Samuel 16:7).

Once he had chosen David, *"Then Samuel took the horn of oil, and anointed him in the midst of his brethren: and the spirit of the Lord came upon David from that day forward"* (I Samuel 16:13). Here it is apparent that Samuel had somehow received additional information provided to him from God, to allow him perfect knowledge for choosing the next king of Israel. But how would he have known?

WHY DID SAMUEL CHOOSE DAVID?

The date of David's birth is not precisely known today, but based upon the sequence of chronological events, many historical authorities conventionally date David's birth as ca. 1040 BCE (Funk & Wagnalls 1984). It is also well known that ancient astrologers often equated the birth of a king, the beginning of new cycles, and changes in government with a conjunction between the planets Jupiter and Saturn. These are the two largest, farthest away, and slowest-moving visible planets within the solar system, and their conjunction is known as the "Great Conjunction" (Lehman 2011). In astronomical terms, a conjunction occurs when two planets have moved into "the same space" by zodiacal degree as seen from Earth. Later on, we will see this conjunction again having importance surrounding the birth of Jesus Christ.

Evidence exists that the seven visible planets, including Jupiter and Saturn, were observed and followed by astrologers as early as 2000 to 1800 BCE. In his studies based upon the known historical evidence, Campion states the following:

Individual fixed stars offered a natural frame of reference for locating planetary position and it appears that, by the Old Babylonian period, perhaps by 1800 BCE, a system had been established which grouped stars according to the calendar; three groups of twelve stars were arranged in three paths across the sky, one based on the celestial equator, one north of it, and the other south (Campion 2008, 40).

Campion goes on to assert that by 1000 BCE, the systematic science of astrology had evolved into "an elaborate rule-based system" that "covered nearly all observable celestial phenomena" (Campion 2008, 43). These evidence-based statements help us identify that astrologers around 1000 BCE, and thus during the time of Samuel and David, would have been able to benefit from these earlier astrological developments. As a descendant of Abraham and member of the Hebrew culture, Samuel would very likely have had access to considerable astrological knowledge regarding the movements of the seven visible planets, the Great Conjunction along with its meaning for humanity, and the grouping of constellations into the twelve divisions of the zodiac.

Based upon the existing astronomical phenomena and other historical events, I now propose the following specific date for the birth of King David: January 31, 1039 BCE. First, it is important to note that this particular date is very nearly identical to the approximate date selected by numerous conventional historical authorities. Second, on this specific date the two planets, Jupiter and Saturn, were exactly conjoined. To Samuel, finding the exact Great Conjunction at the time of David's birth would have surely indicated an essential sign from God identifying David as the next king of Israel. We shall examine in some detail the proposed astrological chart of David momentarily.

THE STAR OF DAVID

At this point, before going further into this investigation, it may be helpful to first introduce a discussion of the Star of David, because certain ambiguous reports within the astrological community regarding its origins have led to many unsupported claims related to David's date of birth. Initially pertaining to King David, the Star of David henceforth became a symbol for Israel and Judaism, continuing through the present day. Just what is the Star of David? Said to have been used as the Shield of David on his coat of arms, the Star of David was also known as the Seal of Solomon. Because he was David's son, Solomon inherited David's coat of arms and traditional symbol.

Historians have theorized that the symbol may have actually arisen due to the double Greek delta in David's name, symbolic for D–V–D (New World Encyclopedia 2015), thereby forming the familiar double-triangle shape.

The Star of David. *Image from Google Public Domain Images.*

On the other hand, there is an unproven assumption by some modern astrologers that the symbol of the Star of David indicated a double interlocking "grand trine" (a concept that will be discussed shortly), forming a hexagram (a six-pointed star) in David's natal horoscope. As you already know, a horoscope is an astronomical map of the heavens at the exact time and place of birth as seen from Earth, and is also known as a birth chart or natal chart. My research on the subject of a hexagram in David's birth chart has not been able to verify this assumption. After an extensive survey, I could not identify a pertinent natal chart that had been discovered, published, or even historically possible showing a hexagram near to his possible time of birth, since this astronomical configuration would be very rare. I therefore had to rule out the possibility of finding a hexagram in David's birth chart.

However, at the time of David's birth, we can unequivocally state that Jewish prophets would most assuredly have viewed the planets as agents of God, they would definitely have been aware of the meaning of the Great Conjunction, and they specifically would have been using a twelve-sign celestial zodiac. But we are not sure whether the natal horoscope itself was in use at the time of David's birth. According to researchers, a natal horoscope or birth chart applying to individuals may not have been developed until around 500 BCE (Campion 2012). Nevertheless, this information does not stop us from constructing a horoscope based on the historical knowledge that we do have today.

We do know that ancient astrologers closely followed major astrological events such as the Great Conjunction. For these prophets and wise men of old, when the Great Conjunction occurred during or just prior to a birth, it would have produced ample evidence and certain proof from God that a king or leader would be born. Thus, the Great Conjunction occurring in 1039 BCE would have allowed Samuel to determine, without any doubt, that David was the next chosen king of Israel.

BASIC CONCEPTS OF THE BIRTH CHART

To prepare us to move forward with some astrological concepts, a discussion of some technical detail over the next few pages is impossible to avoid, and for those readers who are non–astrologers, basic explanations shall be provided as simply as possible. Over the millennia, a specific language and pictorial symbolism were invented in order to describe the many important technical and geometrical ideas inherent in the study of astrology. This is the same type of process that occurred in the development of mathematics and numerous other technical subject matters. It becomes necessary to introduce a certain number of specific terms in the astrological language, but they will be held to a minimum as much as possible.

The great path of the sun, as seen from Earth, forms a giant circle through the zodiac known as the "ecliptic," which forms the basic circular outline of the birth chart. The ecliptic is mathematically divided into 360 equal degrees. The twelve zodiac signs are also equally divided along the ecliptic, with 30 degrees forming each sign. Within this circle, the planets and chart "angles" are then placed at specific points where they are observed along the ecliptic. Thus, the horoscope literally becomes a map of the sky at the time of the nativity or other moment in time that is being observed.

In the natal chart, the term "aspects" applies to the mathematical configurations drawn between the planets and other important chart locations based upon the ordinary geometry of the circle. The major aspect patterns are based upon the 360-degree circle and are computed in the following manner:

Conjunction: 360 degrees divided by *one* forms a "conjunction" aspect, usually considered to be 0 degrees, as the counting of degrees around the circle resumes back at 0. The conjunction combines two individual planets or chart features on or near the same space along the ecliptic. The conjunction indicates a strong focus, emphasis, and concentration of energy.

Opposition: 360 degrees divided by *two* forms an "opposition" aspect of 180 degrees between two planets or chart features placed on opposite sides of the chart. The opposition aspect describes an awareness between two opposing factors, which may either complement one another or present potential conflicts. An emphasis on either balance or competition may be indicated, depending on the rest of the pattern in the entire chart.

Trine: 360 degrees divided by *three* forms a "trine" aspect of 120 degrees. The trine aspect represents an easy flow of energy between the planets or chart features involved in the aspect. Trines indicate a lack of stress and often promote idealism, inspiration, and harmony among the affected areas of the chart.

Square: 360 degrees divided by *four* forms a "square" aspect of 90 degrees. The square aspect indicates areas of challenge, tension, and action. When given an appropriate amount of attention, those potential challenges often lead to areas of intense accomplishment. Squares often show areas of resistance or blockage and may require action, decisions, or a change in initial direction.

Sextile: 360 degrees divided by *six* forms a "sextile" aspect of 60 degrees. The sextile aspect represents affinity, opportunity, and attraction between the planets and areas of the chart involved in the aspect. Sextiles often indicate compatibility and understanding between those areas of the chart.

These aspects are then given an "orb" of allowable distance of influence along the ecliptic from exactitude, usually between 5 and 8 degrees for the major aspects. The smaller the orb, indicating a greater closeness of exactitude, generally provides a greater overall effect, according to the nature of the aspect and the planets involved, as well as to the entire chart pattern. The meaning given to the individual aspects developed over thousands of years in a system of careful observational research.

The chart "angles" are specific positions that are geometrically determined at birth by certain horizontal and vertical lines formed within the great circle of the zodiac, extending outward into space from the exact birth location. The angle known as the "Ascendant" is the point located on the eastern horizon as viewed from the place of birth. Here the Ascendant degree forms the exact place on the ecliptic that *appears* to be rising on the eastern horizon at the time of birth (we know that the Earth is actually rotating, but the geometry works either way). The corresponding opposite angle on the same horizontal axis is known as the "Descendant" and represents the point on the ecliptic located exactly on the western horizon.

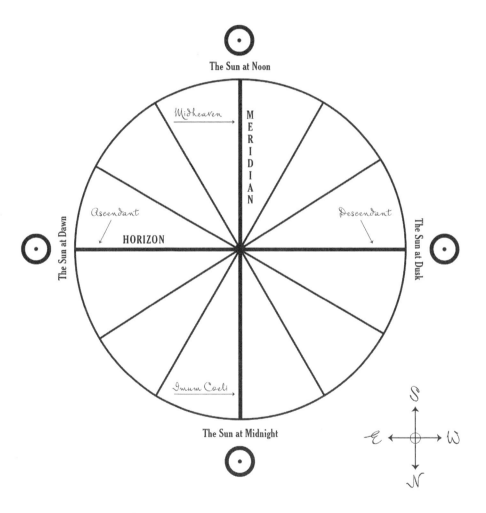

The Natural Horoscope Wheel. *Image from Google Public Domain Images.*

The vertical axis or meridian of the birth chart then forms the angle known as the zenith or "Midheaven," which is the position on the ecliptic that appears to be directly overhead at the time and place of birth. Similarly, its opposite angle, called the "Imum Coeli" or nadir, is the lowest point and is located directly beneath our feet on the opposite side of the Earth.

The four angles are therefore shaped by the great horizontal and vertical axes of the birth chart and are consequently given great importance in astrological interpretation. They form the exact physical locations on the ecliptic that represent the interaction of time and space, at the given moment of birth, ostensibly forming the physical embodiment of the divine act of birth.

THE GRAND TRINE

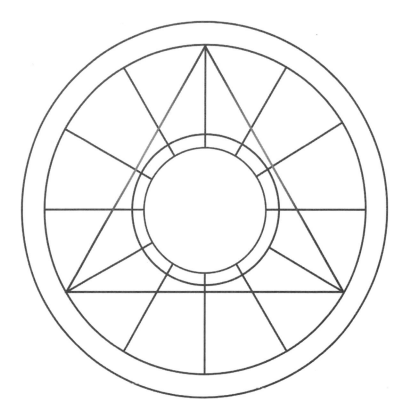

A grand trine

As previously mentioned, the astronomical aspect known as the "trine" is a measurement of 120 degrees between two zodiacal positions on the ecliptic circle forming the outline of the natal chart. Based upon detailed work in astrological history described earlier, we know that the trine and other basic geometrical configurations would have been included within the larger body of astrological knowledge recognized by the Hebrew people during the historical time period surrounding David's birth.

A singular trine is commonly found in a birth chart. A "grand trine," however, is a formation shaped like a large equilateral triangle, which connects three basic trines together into a large formation encompassing the entire chart. Found less frequently, the grand trine is an astrological configuration associated with numerous blessings and great abundance. It is formed in the birth chart when three points (including the sun, moon, planets, and angles or axis of the chart) connect three equal sides of triangle. The planetary bodies or chart points divide the gigantic circle of the celestial zodiac by three, thus forming a giant equilateral triangle in the heavens at the time of birth. We will come back to further discuss this concept momentarily, when reviewing David's chart.

THE GREAT CONJUNCTION

In an effort to further refine David's date of birth, I conducted a detailed computer search that reviewed any possible Great Conjunctions occurring during the approximate time frame deemed appropriate by historians. Approximately every twenty years, the planets Jupiter and Saturn conjoin to form an astrological conjunction, entering the same zodiacal degree or point on the ecliptic, as seen from Earth. During the time of a Great Conjunction, the two planets typically indicate positions of influence in a government or kingdom and were said to represent persons of royalty, the birth and death of kings, and the disposition of important leaders.

For interested readers, a discussion of the Great Conjunction can be found in astrological textbooks (Lehman 2011). In more recent times, this same cycle has been used to help understand the pattern of death and assassinations (or attempted assassinations) of certain US presidents, within specific twenty-year time spans during and before the twentieth century.

Using criteria for an exact Great Conjunction, I set up a horoscope chart for January 31, 1039 BCE, which happens to be the closest Great Conjunction timed to historically match the probable dates suggested by historians for David's birth. It is highly interesting that this chart includes several grand trines involving six planetary bodies plus the angle of the Ascendant (when using an estimated degree in the zodiac sign of Gemini on the Ascendant).

NATAL CHART

Jan 31 1039 BC, Thu
1:42 pm LMT -2:20:48
Bethlehem, Israel
31°N43′ 035°E12′

Geocentric
Tropical
Placidus
True Node

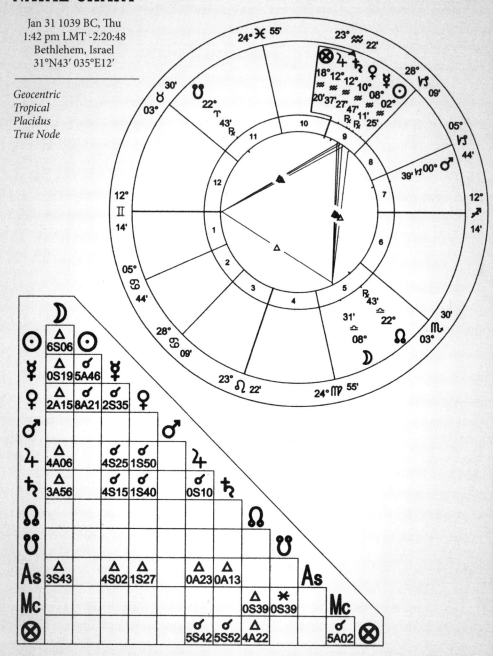

Chart 1: King David (visible planets), *Solar Fire software. v7.0.4*

While the chart for King David does not have the interlocking hexagram specifically shown in the Star of David, the chart nevertheless shows a system of grand trines that include six out of the seven planetary bodies known at that time (the planets Uranus, Neptune, and Pluto are not visible to the naked eye and were not discovered until many centuries later). The chart forms such an extensive system of grand trines within the birth chart, it would indeed have been extremely rare. While not forming a hexagram, it is still possible that the system of numerous grand trines in David's proposed birth horoscope would have helped generate the symbolism seen in David's coat of arms.

As a wise man and prophet of old, following in the footsteps of Abraham and Moses, Samuel would almost surely have been an astrologer. Looking for a sign from God, it is highly reasonable for Samuel to have looked for the Great Conjunction in the chart of the king. Seeing that sign from God at the time of David's birth, Samuel may have chosen David as future king because God gave Samuel this sign from the heavens. The combination of the Great Conjunction with the numerous celestial trines found in the heavens at his time of birth would have promised a multitude of blessings, good fortune, and abundance for the new king and the Jewish people.

THE CHART FITS THE MAN

While trying not to go into excessive detail, and avoiding unnecessary astrological language, let us look briefly at the chart proposed for the birth of David (see chart 1). A list and simplified definition of each of the chart symbols can be found in the appendix. However, any individuals who are not familiar with astrological structure or terminology may wish to skip over any overly technical parts of this section.

Because it was impossible to know the exact time of David's birth, an estimation of the birth time was required. For reasons described below, the zodiacal degree of 12 Gemini is used for the Ascendant, the angle on the eastern horizon (located on the left-hand side of the chart) for the date of January 31, 1039 BCE. In this manner, astrologers and students can study the character of David associated with the suggested horoscope.

It is, of course, not really historically possible to know David's exact moment of birth. Nevertheless, using the suggested time of birth will determine a plausible Ascendant that can bring the legendary character of the man and the factually recorded events of his life into sharper focus. As we shall see, using the proposed Ascendant as a tool will clearly link together many of the known historical facts of his life with his personality. These links can then be examined with greater clarity and will add enormous perspective to our study of the man named David.

Using only the visible planets and the suggested Ascendant on the date of the Great Conjunction, the chart shows six planetary bodies that form an extensive system of five grand trines. All the planetary bodies and the Ascendant are located in the "element" of air. The elements are a basic astrological concept that identify certain core characteristics with their associated zodiac signs. The element of air especially pertains to the development of keen perception and individual powers of judgment, arbitration, intelligence, intuition, and interpersonal communication. This astrological element includes the zodiac signs of Gemini, Libra, and Aquarius. Note that the definition in modern chemistry for the word "element" means something entirely different today, but the word originated from ancient astrology.

This astounding number of grand trines involves the sun, Mercury, Venus, Jupiter, and Saturn, all of which are grouped in the sign of Aquarius, along with the moon in Libra, and the Ascendant in Gemini. (For basic discussions or for further study of the zodiac signs, planetary aspects, elements, and other astrological concepts, please review the listings shown in the appendix.)

Each of the five planetary bodies grouped in Aquarius is forming a separate grand-trine formation, separated by about 120 geometrical degrees between both the moon and the Ascendant, and encompassing the entire chart. As noted earlier, however, this series of grand trines does not form a hexagram, or six-sided star, which could not have been astronomically possible at any time surrounding David's potential date of birth.

Chart 2 includes the modern chart placements. Contemporary astrologers may want to include the planet Pluto, located just above the Ascendant, in this grouping of grand trines, but Pluto would obviously not have been visible by eye during the time of Samuel.

David was described as "one of those peculiarly favored beings who quickly win the favor of all with whom they come into contact" (Kent 1908, 125). In the astrological birth chart, trines in particular are known to confer grace and harmony to the personality, and exceptional good luck throughout life. From historical records and descriptions in the books of Samuel, it is evident that David had a genius for mediation, was able to command diverse tribal allegiances, and was skillful as a moderator, arbitrator, and diplomat (Gunn 2001).

He had a keen sense of justice, great courage, generosity, a pleasing and handsome demeanor, and great moral sensibility. "He was naturally gifted with a rare grace and winsomeness," yet even more importantly for the Hebrew people, "the greatness and breadth of his character were demonstrated by his repentance. . . . The sight of a conquering monarch humbly confessing his sins was unprecedented" (Kent 1908, 163–164).

NATAL CHART

Jan 31 1039 BC, Thu
1:42 pm LMT -2:20:48
Bethlehem, Israel
31°N43′ 035°E12′

Geocentric
Tropical
Placidus
True Node

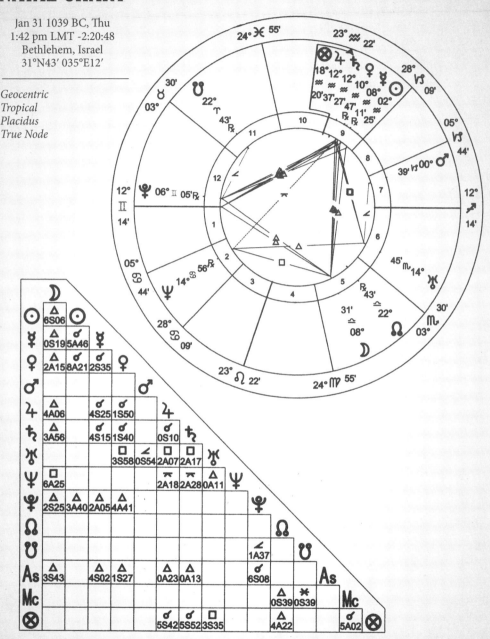

Chart 2: King David (modern planets), *Solar Fire software. v7.0.4*

These statements are particularly well represented by the horoscope's grand trines in air, and further, through the planetary "dignities" as well as the exact Great Conjunction of Jupiter-Saturn shown in David's chart. The system of planetary dignities and exaltations in astrology is based upon a planet's "rulership" or affinity for a certain zodiacal sign. Over the ages, the traditional dignities were based on actual observations of how well a particular planet was observed to operate in human affairs when placed in any given sign.

Still being used today, planets are said to have greater or lesser strength or dignity when placed in certain specific signs. The combination of the model or archetypal nature of the planet, along with the sign in which it is located, creates a blend that clearly influences the manner in which that particular planet tends to operate. Any planet exalted or dignified by sign position will have more power, seem to operate more smoothly, and become "lifted up" by the sign in which it is located.

Placed in the zodiacal sign of Aquarius, the Great Conjunction is highly and doubly dignified. The planet Saturn is located in its traditional sign of rulership (the sign of Aquarius). The dignified Saturn in David's chart indicates his increased awareness, tolerance, and drive toward a higher level of social responsibility. As king, he became an authority figure who was greatly beloved by the Hebrew people through his friendship with and acceptance of all the various tribes of Israel. With his kingship, David succeeded in forming a convergence and consolidation of the various conflicting tribal and economic allegiances and interests.

Similarly, the planet Jupiter in David's horoscope is dignified by placement in the ninth "house." The diurnal house system is a basic system for dividing the chart into twelve sections, or areas of significant personal meaning and relevance in that person's life, and is based upon the exact time of day at birth. For further study, astrologer Sue Tompkins gives an excellent description of the house system (Tompkins 2006). Jupiter in David's ninth-house division indicates a particularly strong ability to reach out to others in the role of judge, religious mentor, or educator and represents a person who possesses great generosity of judicial spirit, religious ardor, personal character, integrity, and clarity.

Adding a third and additional level of dignity is the position of the Great Conjunction culminating near the zenith or highest point of the natal chart. Note that the Great Conjunction would have been nearly directly overhead at the proposed time of David's birth. Moreover, the Great Conjunction is found to be within "orb" (within the allowable number of degrees) of conjunction with Venus, the sun, and Mercury, the planetary ruler of the sign on the Ascendant. Both Venus and Jupiter are considered to be the most "benefic" planets in the solar system, usually providing enormous goodness, advantage, and idealism in any area that they touch within the horoscope.

These five planets form a significant grouping that focuses on the ninth house, known to astrologers as the most religious division of the chart. The ninth-house emphasis is associated with topics of the utmost importance in David's life; these topics include faith, religion, the law, justice, and, most especially, his understanding and relationship with God. This placement indicates a strong probability for certain profound questions that David may have been asking throughout his life. Such questions might include "What is my relationship with God? Who or what is God? What is right and wrong?" (Tompkins 2006, 227).

AN EXALTED MARS

Mars is another highly dignified planet in David's natal chart. His exalted Mars in the zodiac sign of Capricorn speaks to David's skill with the sword, his great courage, and his success *"as a mighty valiant man, and a man of war, and prudent in matters, and a comely person"* (I Samuel 16:18). David met great success in everything that he attempted to do, leading to public acclaim that *"the Lord is with him"* in all things.

Yet we also know that David was not without sin. His exalted Mars has a major aspect with only one other planet, that of a square (90-degree angle) with the moon. Although the orb is a little wide (about 8 degrees), the square would still have been effective and represents difficulty concerning his relationships with women.

An extremely high amount of sexual tension would have been generated from this exalted Mars. Even more sexual tension would have been formulated from the angular position of Mars in the seventh house, the house section pertaining directly to personal relationships. Within this astrological setting, the archetypal Mars energy can easily be linked to the story of David's unbridled passion toward Bathsheba.

As the story goes, upon viewing Bathsheba bathing on a neighboring rooftop, David ordered his men to kill Uriah, Bathsheba's husband, for the sole purpose of making her his own wife. For these deeds, David experienced the displeasure of the Lord, for *"the thing that David had done displeased the Lord"* (2 Samuel 11:27), resulting in the eventual death of the first child produced by David and Bathsheba's union. For his part, David then bore great repentance toward the Lord.

Having David's astrological chart helps us understand what was going on at this point in David's life. For a man who had everything in life that anyone could possibly desire, including leadership of the house of Judah, succession to the throne of Israel, a great military reputation, a remarkable comeliness of demeanor, an unmatched physical prowess, and enormous spiritual blessings from God, why would this deeply religious man risk the wrath of God? Why would he kill Bathsheba's husband in order to take possession of this one woman, when he already had several other highly desirable wives?

David's actions only make sense when seen in the astrological context of an exalted Mars, gifted with the enormous sexual energy flowing through its placement in the powerful and angular seventh house, combined with its square to the moon, providing difficult obstacles blocking his path regarding relationships with women. Clearly, Bathsheba's marriage to Uriah was an obstacle that David felt compelled to remove.

Within the universal astrological archetypes, Mars is understood as the principle of assertive sexual urge, the impulse to act, and sexual chase and conquest. While Mars in Capricorn can potentially indicate self-control, Mars in the seventh-house placement, as seen in David's chart, indicates how he approached relationships: with cunning, volatility, outstanding desire, and the intense urge to find a mate.

THE ARIES POINT

It is vitally important to add that David's Mars was located at 0 degrees in a "cardinal" sign. The term "cardinal" corresponds to the four cardinal (prime) directions of east, west, north, and south, pertaining to the four angles of the natural zodiac. The cardinal quality is used in astrology to indicate remarkable ardor, energy, enthusiasm, and ambition.

It is also highly significant that his position of Mars was in exact conjunction with an "Aries Point." An exceedingly potent position, the Aries Point is located at 0 degrees of the four cardinal signs (Aries, Cancer, Libra, and Capricorn). The Aries Point is succinctly described here by astrologer Noel Tyl (italics were included by Tyl):

> It is extremely sensitive to involvement with any planet or other point or other midpoint by conjunction. . . . When the Aries Point is activated in a personal horoscope, *there is the potential of public projection for the person in terms of the planet, point, or midpoint configured with it* (Tyl 2009, 312).

Talk about public projection! It goes without saying how forcefully in magnitude the placement on the Aries Point seems to have activated David's cardinal Mars. The resulting complex of tremendous Mars energy is exalted, cardinal, "angular" (a concept in astrology denoting even more power by placement near one of the chart's angles) and is located exactly on an Aries Point.

This complex is extremely unique in David's chart. Great biblical stories of David's exploits, including the anointment by Samuel, the battle with Goliath, the descriptions of physical prowess, and the story of Bathsheba, are exceptionally well known throughout the Judeo-Christian tradition even today, some 3,000 years later. This is a vital part of David's legacy to the world.

THE PSALMIST

Nonetheless, we also know that David was a great lover of song, a poet, a renowned musician, and a psalmist of great talent. This description can be directly confirmed in the horoscope through the positions of Venus, Mercury (ruler of the Ascendant), and the sun, all of which are found in conjunction with one another, trine to the Ascendant, and in trine aspect with the moon. The moon, in turn, is located in the creative fifth-house placement. These positions form part of the system of grand trines mentioned earlier.

The zodiac sign where the moon is placed is Libra, the sign of beauty and harmony, and ruled by Venus. Therefore, we find a significantly strong position of Venus in David's chart. This is often the case in the charts of talented musicians and artists. Both the planetary positions by house, along with the interplanetary aspects in David's chart, confirm great talent in lyrical harmony and exceptional artistic or poetical inspiration. Thus, in many ways, the magnificent trine aspects and other fortunate planetary placements in David's chart signify multiple blessings; a superb ease of expression, poetic, and lyrical accomplishment; and an enormous facilitation, all of which are found to be historically present in David's life.

It is said that many of the songs and praises in the book of Psalms were written by David. Perhaps he wrote some of the Psalms that we mentioned in earlier chapters. Whether or not it was David, clearly the Psalmist praises God for providing the heavens, the lights, and the stars, and for an amazing array of nightly knowledge, all found to be so significant in David's life. For who alone among mankind can look upon the magnificent solar system and starry heavens and not see the mighty handiwork of God?

THE TIMING IN DAVID'S LIFE

We do not know David's age at the time of his anointment by Samuel, which may have occurred at a very young age. We also do not know David's age when he entered Saul's court with his harp as a musician to comfort Saul. Even when he fought the battle against Goliath, only the three eldest brothers, out of a total of seven older male siblings, followed Saul into battle. Apparently, there were four additional brothers older than David who were also considered too young to fight in battle. When counting the tribes of Israel in the book of Numbers, Moses was known to count only the males *"from twenty years old and upward, all that are able to go forth to war in Israel"* (Numbers 1:2–3). From this information, we can deduce that David must have had four brothers older than himself who were not yet twenty years of age.

During the battle with Goliath, David's brothers tried to turn him away because of his young age. The armor of Saul was too large and did not fit David, and he was described as a youth on all these occasions.

The date that Saul initially became king is not absolutely clear, but it is generally thought that Saul served as the first king of Israel for about fifteen years, ranging from 1025 until 1010 BCE (Carr and Conway 2010). If we accept David's date of birth in January 1039 BCE, then it follows that he had to be twenty-nine years old when he first ascended to the throne upon the death of Saul. Historians believe that David served as king for forty years, until the date of his own death in 970 BCE (Carr and Conway 2010).

There are several methods used in astrology for the timing of events and to assist in the confirmation of an estimated birth chart. One of these methods is the use of transiting planets through the solar system. The horoscope marks the location of the planets at the time of birth. As the planets continue to revolve around the sun, their continuing movements are called "transits." The zodiacal placements of the transiting planets are then compared with the natal chart in order to examine how these new placements are related to the original birth chart.

One particularly important and highly significant transit is known as the "Saturn Return." As Saturn revolves around the solar system, it generally takes twenty-eight to thirty years in order to complete its revolution and return to its original placement in the zodiac as found at the time of birth. The Saturn Return is a transit that occurs with every person who lives long enough to be within that age group. It is a cyclic pattern long considered by astrologers to be a highly significant time of greater individual understanding, responsibility, and maturity as one grows older in life.

Using the suggested horoscope for David, his Saturn Return would have occurred in the year 1010 BCE, exactly coinciding with the historical date of his ascension to king. As the archetypal planet of responsibility, discipline, and maturity, the Saturn Return indicates a person's ability to develop into his greatest potential and to reap what he has sown. For David, his greatest potential was to become a great leader, judge,

and king over Israel. As transiting Saturn returned to its highly dignified natal position in David's chart, he stepped into this exalted new role.

The exact timing of the Saturn Return therefore acts to confirm that the suggested horoscope for David is likely correct. There are several other methods used in astrology to confirm or rectify an estimated birth chart in order to provide a more exact time of birth. However, a discussion of that methodology is more advanced, fairly complex, and beyond the scope of this book.

As we look through David's chart, there are too many outstanding "coincidences" and correspondences between his horoscope, his personality, and the events of his life to be considered merely random chance. I believe the deep rational structure and correspondence among all these factors provide profound spiritual evidence of a wonderful and divine order to the universe.

Just as Samuel used astrology to help determine that David would become a great leader and king of Israel, so I believe that astrology is the celestial signature from God to assist in the illumination and knowledge of humanity. This concept has been proven through the use of biblical scripture. Astrology can be used to assist in our capacity to understand profound archetypal meanings and to provide knowledge on how those meanings can deeply affect the individual. Most importantly, it can be used to expand the individual's comprehension of his purpose in life itself. Consequently, astrology can be used to assist in greater spiritual understanding, and can provide a more thorough realization of both the gifts and the burdens that were put in place by God for each individual to bear throughout life. We will continue to explore these concepts in greater depth in later chapters, and as we turn to the use of astrology in the New Testament.

Chapter VIII

WISE MEN AND THE STAR OF BETHLEHEM

As we weave together many of the passages found in the New Testament, let us also remember the discussions regarding the natural worldview, a way of looking at the world that was universally in place during the historical time frame surrounding the birth of Christ. In this worldview, the astronomical signs were seen as messages sent from the heavens above to announce God's intentions for human beings here below. As we have demonstrated, the ancient Jewish people assuredly believed that celestial signs reflected God's will. This belief continued on through antiquity and into the centuries surrounding the arrival of Christianity. Many passages in the New Testament witness the continuation of the same worldview.

WISE MEN SEEK JESUS

Much has been written about the nature of wisdom in the Old Testament. But in the New Testament, only the gospel of Matthew mentions the wise men who have come to seek Jesus.

> *Now when Jesus was born in Bethlehem of Judea in the days of Herod the king,* *behold, there came wise men from the east to Jerusalem, Saying, Where is he that* *is born King of the Jews? For we have seen his star in the east, and are come to* *worship him* (Matthew 2:1–2).

Who are these wise men? In the classic work on the life of Christ by Giovanno Papini, we learn that the wise men most likely came from Chaldea, mounted on camels, and "were guided to Judea by a new star like a comet, which appears every so often in the sky to announce the birth of a prophet or the death of a Caesar." Papini continues, "They were not kings, these wise men, but in Media and Persia, the wise men directed the kings. . . . In the midst of a people sunk in material things, they represented the spirit" (Papini 1970, 14). Surely, the wise men were holy men, and as such, they were the first of their kind to venerate the newborn infant Jesus.

When the wise men went before Herod, they recounted how they had been led by a star to seek the King of Judea. "Seeing that the astrologers did not come back to tell him the place where the new nephew of David had appeared, he [Herod] ordered that all the boy babies of Bethlehem be killed" (Papini 1970, 14).

In these passages, Papini clearly concludes that the wise men were astrologers who represented the spirit of God. There is no other logical explanation possible: God intentionally made the Star of Bethlehem for this purpose, as a sign to the world for the birth of Jesus and for the wise men to follow.

When Herod the king heard of these events, he certainly paid attention to the sayings of the wise men.

> *Then Herod, when he had privily called the wise men, inquired of them diligently what time the star appeared. And he sent them to Bethlehem. . . . When they had heard the king, they departed; and, lo, the star, which they saw in the east, went before them, till it came and stood over where the young child was. When they saw the star, they rejoiced with exceeding great joy* (Matthew 2:7, 9–10).

To this day, Christians everywhere annually celebrate the birth of Jesus Christ with a reenactment of this scene, in which the wise men follow the Christ star, bearing gifts to worship the newborn child. Yet, there has been controversy among biblical scholars over the exact date of birth of Jesus and what astrological or astronomical event actually produced the Star of Bethlehem. More detail on this subject will be discussed shortly.

IN THE WORDS OF JESUS

It is written in the Bible that Jesus spoke many words of parable and prophesy. When prophesizing on the future of Jerusalem, Jesus himself spoke of watching for signs to be found in the heavens above and repeated some of the very same words that were written in Genesis. As written in the book of Luke, Jesus said:

> And there shall be signs in the sun, and in the moon, and in the stars; and upon the Earth distress of nations, with perplexity; the sea and the waves roaring. . . . And when these things begin to come to pass, then look up, and lift up your heads; for your redemption draweth nigh. And he spoke to them a parable; Behold the fig tree, and all the trees; When they now shoot forth, ye see and know of your own selves that summer is now nigh at hand. So likewise ye, when ye see these things come to pass, know ye that the kingdom of God is nigh at hand (Luke 21: 25, 28–31).

Just as we were told in Genesis, Jesus now tells us again that there shall be signs in the heavens emanating from God, and they are available for all of humanity to view and understand. According to these scriptures, Jesus clearly directs the apostles to seek knowledge from the celestial signs. Moreover, Jesus specifically mentions that signs shall be found in the sun, in the moon, and in the stars. This instruction comes to the apostles directly from Jesus, so it behooves us today to pay close attention. The signs must be a significant and powerful tool, and they must be tremendously important in the search for knowledge from God.

IN THE WORDS OF PAUL

The apostle Paul, too, celebrates the glory of the heavens when he says:

> There are also celestial bodies, and bodies terrestrial: but the glory of the celestial is one, and the glory of the terrestrial is another. There is one glory of the sun, and another glory of the moon, and another glory of the stars: for one star differeth from another star in glory. . . . And as we have borne the image of the earthy, we shall also bear the image of the heavenly (1 Corinthians 15:40–4, 49).

These statements are really quite extraordinary and relate most directly to astrology. For when astrologers draw a person's natal horoscope, they are literally making an exact written copy of the heavens, as seen from Earth, at the precise moment and place of birth. As Paul has said, *"we shall also bear the image of the heavenly"* here on Earth. The image of the heavenly really *is* the natal horoscope. The image from God is imprinted on the newborn infant at the moment of birth. Here Paul teaches us that the image of

84

the heavenly is a glory offered to mankind from God. And in the same manner indicated by Paul, astrology shall be employed to view the glorious signs provided by God. Astrology thus represents a systematic method to attain wisdom, as we search for God's will within our lives here on Earth. What could be more simple than that?

DETERMINING THE BIRTH OF CHRIST

It is unfortunate that the actual date of birth of Jesus Christ to this day remains obscure. There are probably just as many suggested dates for Christ's birth as there are investigators. Researchers have employed many different techniques in efforts to discover the exact date. For instance, some researchers have examined the calendar of taxation dates, because paying taxes was a possible historical reason that Joseph, being of the house of David, was required to travel to Bethlehem. Other researchers have suggested that Joseph and Mary were unable to find a room at the inn due to a Jewish Holy Day occurring around the same time, thus basing their observations on a review of the Holy Days.

Some investigators have reviewed the occurrence of comets and other possible astronomical data linked to the Star of Bethlehem phenomenon, and have suggested plausible reasons for the star's brilliant appearance. One such hypothesis conjectures that the exact joining together or conjunction of the two brightest planets in the solar system, Venus and Jupiter, would have resulted in an exceptionally brilliant display. Another hypothesis links the planet Venus in conjunction instead with a bright star of the night sky.

During my review, I was able to find numerous suggested dates of birth in a range from 7 to 2 BCE. This is a fairly wide range encompassing approximately five years. However, we do know that the birth occurred during Herod's reign of Jerusalem. Since historians have closely dated Herod's death to the spring of 4 BCE, common sense tells us that the birth of Jesus had to occur before Herod died (Gill 2017). Therefore, some of the above suggested dates do not work.

After much review, the historical researcher who in my opinion most diligently examined all the available data and put the data together in the most logical fashion is Colin Humphreys, PhD. A professor at the University of Cambridge, Professor Humphreys wrote a treatise that is at once brilliant, scholarly, authoritative, and intriguing, simply titled *The Star of Bethlehem* (Humphreys 1994). I encourage any readers wanting to delve deeper into this subject to review the Humphreys study directly for themselves. Please allow me to briefly outline his reasoning with the facts and details as he presented them in the treatise referenced above. All subsequent references to Professor Humphreys work have been obtained from this source.

The Star of Bethlehem According to Professor Colin Humphreys

First, Professor Humphreys states that some modern theologians and historical researchers simply decided to ignore the Star of Bethlehem story or have otherwise determined that it was beyond the bounds of scientific explanation. But he goes on to comment that in such cases, it is still most desirable to consider a working hypothesis in which the star is indeed considered to be a real astronomical object, in order to more fully investigate any natural phenomenon that could possibly correspond to the biblical narrative.

Even so, Humphreys remarks that the difficulty in treating the star as a real astronomical object is considerable and should not be underestimated, due to several of the following reasons. In the scriptures, the star was said to have arisen in the East and guided the wise men (consistently referred to as magi by Humphreys) to Jerusalem. After the magi left Herod in Jerusalem, then the star evidently turned south and went ahead of them toward Bethlehem, until it finally stood still over the house in Bethlehem where the young child was located. How could such an unusual astronomical event occur? And why was it not recorded more clearly in astronomical history?

While the earliest known account of the Star of Bethlehem comes from the gospel of Matthew (as found in Matthew 2:1–12), Humphreys states that most scholars believe that the actual text of Matthew was not finally written until about 80 CE, quite a number of years later. The fact that the wise men or magi followed the star to Jerusalem indicates that it was not a normal or routine astronomical event. Humphreys includes additional detailed information on the history of the magi and corroborates that at the time, they were considered valuable members of the royal Babylonian court and did indeed study a combination of astronomy and astrology.

Ever since the sixth century BCE, during the time of Nebuchadnezzar and the exile of Daniel, Humphreys reports there was a strong Jewish colony existing in Babylonia. He states it is therefore quite likely that the magi were familiar with the Jewish prophecies of a Savior or Messiah. Humphreys concludes that the magi who followed the Star of Bethlehem were astrologers, were familiar with the Jewish prophecies, and most probably came from Arabia or Mesopotamia, as it was told in Matthew.

Humphreys reports that he discovered numerous references in ancient literature regarding visits by the magi to kings and emperors in other countries for the purpose of paying homage. Consequently, a visit by the magi to pay homage to the new "king of the Jews" was not unusual within that context. Humphreys then asserts that there must have been a clear and unmistakable astronomical or astrological message that occurred to start the magi on their journey.

At this point in his treatise, Humphreys systematically reviews every type of physical or astronomical object that could have caused the Star of Bethlehem event. He examines anything that might have been possible, or anything that was likely to have occurred, within the historical time frame for the birth of Jesus. He comes to one final conclusion: The astronomical object known as the Star of Bethlehem could only have been a comet.

Comets are easily visible to the naked eye, can last for several weeks or even months at a time, can be extremely bright, are highly dramatic in appearance, and can move either slowly or quickly across the sky. Humphreys states that comets can typically move 1 or 2 zodiacal degrees per day through the celestial sphere, relative to our view from Earth. Through a complex examination of the astronomical data, Humphreys also identifies that the magi initially saw the comet in the East in the zodiac sign of Capricorn.

He goes on to document the length of time it would have taken the magi, after seeing the comet, to leave Babylon, travel by camel, and arrive in Bethlehem. Specifically, Humphreys suggests that this journey would have been between 550 miles, using a harder, direct route, and 900 miles, using an easier, indirect route. He then states it would likely have taken one to two months of fairly leisurely travel. The same trip was historically undertaken by Nebuchadnezzar in as little as twenty-three days, when traveling the route with little delay.

Humphreys provides further documentation that a fully loaded camel can cover fifty miles per day if traveling fairly comfortably. Therefore, it is highly reasonable to suggest that the range of time for the magi to undertake a journey from Babylon to Bethlehem occurred in a time frame as little as twenty-three days, and up to one or possibly two months.

But how could the comet have turned toward the south and then stood over Bethlehem? Humphreys writes that from our point of view on Earth, the comet looked as if it changed direction on its way out from perihelion (the point at which it was nearest the sun) and thus appeared to change directions from east to south (moving toward the equator). Its next eventual movement would have been toward the west. Amazingly, and for legitimate scientific and astronomical reasons, a comet can appear to move forward, stop, and then change direction. This is similar to a concept in astrology known as retrograde motion, where an object in orbit around the sun appears to move in forward motion, stop, and then move in apparent backward motion, as seen from our vantage point on Earth. Of course, we know that a comet or planet does not truly move backward, but it might appear to do so from our earthly viewpoint.

Humphreys writes that similar language identifying that a comet was "standing over" a location has previously been found in the contemporaneous literature of that time period. For example, in 64 CE Josephus wrote that another "star" (most likely a comet) resembling a sword had "stood over" the city of Jerusalem. Comets were frequently described as swords during this time frame due to their upward tails, which pointed in a direction away from the sun. The tail in the Star of Bethlehem may also have been seen as pointing in a direction to be taken by the magi.

Professor Humphreys affirms that according to generally accepted scientific knowledge, the only possible astronomical object that could have occurred according to the description written in the biblical scriptures is a comet. He then cites evidence of historical records in which comets were associated with good news and the birth of great kings, or even the "sweeping clean" of the old order of things (because the tail of the comet appeared to look like a broom).

Next, in a review of astronomical journals from China, Humphreys provides evidence of detailed and careful records kept by the Chinese people regarding visible comets and other important astronomical events. Humphreys cites undisputed documentation that ancient Chinese observers cataloged a visible comet, which was observed to begin on March 9, 5 BCE, and lasted for over seventy days. A comet lasting for this length of time would have been visible for a long enough period of time to allow the magi sufficient time to travel by camel from Babylon to Jerusalem, and then onward to their final destination in Bethlehem. Only one or two other comets were documented by Chinese observers around this time period, but none of these other comets were able to meet the necessary historical and astronomical criteria.

Due to the specific time frame when the comet was observed and documented in China, Humphreys concludes that the birth of Christ must have occurred between the dates of March 9 and May 4 in 5 BCE. In addition, Humphreys provides other compelling reasons that the magi were watching the sky for a sign of the impending birth of the Jewish king. Those reasons will be described below.

The Timing of Celestial Events

Two other celestial signs from heaven had already appeared. First, a Great Conjunction of Jupiter and Saturn (a cyclical pattern that occurs every twenty years and was previously observed during the birth of King David) had happened three times during the year 7 BCE. Note that a conjunction or other planetary aspect can take place repeatedly when the planets undergo apparent retrograde motion as viewed from Earth. This astronomical phenomenon occurs due to the angle of our view from Earth regarding the planet's orbit around the sun.

The time frame for this series of the Great Conjunction was about one and a half to two years prior to the birth of Christ. As the planets moved in apparent retrograde motion, the Great Conjunction series occurred at the following degrees or measurements on the circle of the ecliptic: The initial conjunction occurred at 20 degrees in the sign of Pisces, the middle conjunction occurred at 17 degrees Pisces, and the final conjunction occurred at 15 degrees Pisces. The importance of these placements will become more apparent as we continue. Remember that traditionally, a Great Conjunction has been shown by astrologers and biblical prophets to coincide with the birth of kings and other great leaders of nations.

Second, an astronomical massing of three planets occurred in February in the following year of 6 BCE. The massing included the planets Mars, Jupiter, and Saturn, also in the sign of Pisces. Called the "Grand Conjunction," the massing of these three planets occurs roughly every 805 years (and by definition includes a Great Conjunction plus the planet Mars). According to Professor Humphreys, Johannes Kepler later calculated that the massing of these three planets in the Grand Conjunction likely occurred during certain other highly significant events in history, including the birth of Moses in 1617 BCE and the birth of the prophet Isaiah in 812 BCE.

While both the Great Conjunction and the Grand Conjunction occurred about one to two years prior to the birth of Jesus, Humphreys speculates that they confirmed to the magi the impending birth of the Messiah. As we have already documented, the third celestial sign appeared as the brilliant comet in March of 5 BCE.

Amazingly, on nearly the identical date as the emergence of the comet, a fourth extremely significant celestial sign occurred. A solar eclipse at exactly 15 degrees of Pisces, precisely the same degree as the final Great Conjunction, took place on March 8, 5 BCE. Additionally, in what could only have been considered a fifth celestial sign from God, the very bright conjunction of the planets Venus and Jupiter also became exact on March 9, 5 BCE. Ultimately, as a result of the overwhelming number of celestial signs emanating from heaven, the magi were finally ready to make their long-awaited journey.

The Roman Census

Critics may bring up a problem with the timing of the Roman census, in which some researchers have conjectured that taxation was the primary reason for Joseph to have traveled with Mary to Bethlehem. Humphreys states that there were actually various types of censuses that occurred during this historical time frame, both for taxation purposes and for purposes of allegiance to Caesar Augustus. Humphreys reports that while some translations of Luke refer to taxation, the purpose of taxation was actually neither stated nor implied in the earlier Greek text from which the translations were made. Humphreys suggests that in some New Testament texts, a mistranslation may have occurred to indicate taxation, but in reality, no taxation was involved at all.

A reading of the same text in the New King James Version confirms Humphreys' statements. The publishers of the New King James Version state that a new translation was necessary in order to present a more complete and more equivalent representation of the original text, in effect, utilizing the "principle of complete equivalence" to ensure the best possible translation became available (Holy Bible, New King James Version). Their corrected reading is shown below:

> And it came to pass in those days that a decree went out from Caesar Augustus that all the world should be registered. This census first took place while Quirinius was governing Syria. So all went to be registered, everyone to his own city. Joseph also went up from Galilee, out of the city of Nazareth, into Judea, to the city of David, which is called Bethlehem, because he was of the house and lineage of David, to be registered with Mary, his betrothed wife, who was with child (Luke 2:1–5).

For additional confirmation, Humphreys mentions that other early historians, including Orosius and Josephus, documented that a Roman census of allegiance and list of births occurred about one year prior to the death of Herod. Historians have already established that Herod died in the spring of 4 BCE; this additional evidence strongly supports the birth of Christ occurring one year earlier than the death of Herod, or in March 5 BCE.

Another important issue may be the length of time that Joseph and Mary stayed in Bethlehem before fleeing to Egypt. Again, according to Professor Humphreys, several essential events had to occur before the family could leave the area. First, according to Jewish law, the circumcision of a male infant occurs seven days after birth (on the eighth day when inclusively counting the date of birth).

Next, the presentation of the young child at the temple in Jerusalem would have occurred forty days after the date of birth. At this point, the date is now getting very close to the date on which Passover fell in 5 BCE, which was April 20. Humphreys states that during Passover, Joseph and all other adult males were required to attend the temple in Jerusalem. Therefore, the departure for Egypt would have been significantly delayed after the birth of Jesus, and this time frame corresponds directly to the length of time needed by the magi to travel to Bethlehem.

We are told in Matthew 2:11 that when the wise men finally arrived in Bethlehem, they located the young child with Mary in a house. It probably took them less than a day of additional travel from Jerusalem to Bethlehem after leaving Herod's court, a distance of only about ten to twelve miles. The family had apparently moved from the manger to a more suitable accommodation and into a house, due to having a substantial amount of business to take care of before they could leave the Bethlehem area. Certainly, there was an adequate amount of time for the journey of the magi to have taken place, after the comet had first appeared on March 9, but before the flight of Joseph away from the despicable reach of Herod, which could not have occurred for at least forty days after the birth.

Throughout this chapter, I have tried to summarize a significant amount of detailed information concerning the accurate timing of the birth of Jesus. A great deal of the information was taken from the superb scholarly treatise documented and written by Professor Colin Humphreys. Even more details concerning the time frame surrounding the birth of Jesus can be found embedded within his paper. I sincerely hope that my summary of his work is adequate to do him justice and will spur readers on to do their own continued investigations. The astrological implications related to the timing and importance of these historical events will be examined in greater detail within the next chapter.

Chapter IX

TIMING AND ASTROLOGY IN THE NEW TESTAMENT

In the scripture of Matthew, it is told that after consulting with Herod, the wise men continued on their journey to Bethlehem, ultimately finding the house where Jesus lay. There they worshiped the young child, presented him with gifts, and then departed directly from Bethlehem into their own country. However, Herod had particularly instructed the wise men to return to court and report on their findings. By not doing as he had instructed, Herod concluded the wise men had mocked him. At this point, the wrathful Herod issued a pervasive decree to murder all the young boys in Bethlehem, *"from two years old and under, according to the time which he had diligently inquired of the wise men"* (Matthew 2:16). It was around this small window of time, just after the departure of the wise men but before the decree had taken place, that Joseph received his prophetic dream to flee into Egypt with the baby Jesus.

Hence, we must ask, what knowledge did Herod receive from the wise men for him to have chosen to exterminate young children at that exact age of two years and under, rather than only the newborn children? The ages chosen by Herod make absolutely no sense whatsoever, unless the wise men provided him specific information regarding the timing of the Great Conjunction (involving the planets Jupiter and Saturn). We know that the Great Conjunction occurred between the months of May and December in 7 BCE. At the time of Herod's decree, which most likely took place in April of 5 BCE, he wanted to ensure that every single male child who could have been born during the period of the Great Conjunction was eliminated.

After conferring with the wise men concerning the timing of their visit, it becomes increasingly evident that Herod was fully cognizant of the meaning of the Great Conjunction. To Herod, any of the Hebrew children born under the Great Conjunction could be considered a potential threat to him or his heirs as a future king of the Jews. Clearly, at the time of his decree, this time period covered just under two years.

ASTROLOGICAL TIMING FOR THE BIRTH OF JESUS CHRIST

Now that we have reliable, corroborative evidence regarding the historical time frame surrounding the comet that became known as the Star of Bethlehem, the visit of the wise men, and Herod's decree, we can work to determine more specific timing for the birth of Jesus Christ. The scriptures tell us that Jesus was born as a human infant under the condition of immaculate conception. Jesus lived a life on Earth that embodied a profound and interwoven union of divine spirit, deep human suffering, priceless service to humanity, and unsurpassed love for God.

On March 8, 5 BCE, a solar eclipse occurred at 15 degrees Pisces. We noticed that this zodiacal degree is exactly the same degree that occurred with the final Great Conjunction in 7 BCE. Throughout history, solar eclipses have traditionally been linked to indicate events of great magnitude to humanity. The fact that this eclipse occurred on precisely the same degree as the Great Conjunction should be deemed *extremely* significant. Especially to the wise men, no other time frame for the birth of Christ could be considered more expressive.

According to this information on timing, and keeping in mind the highly powerful nature of the eclipse chart (to be described in greater detail within the following pages), it is my view that Jesus Christ was born on or near the precise moment of the solar eclipse, which occurred on March 8, 5 BCE, at 7:10:34 a.m., in the location of Bethlehem. I further propose that the comet known as the Star of Bethlehem first appeared in the sky overhead on or near the same moment of birth, as a deeply meaningful announcement to the world proclaiming his birth.

From Professor Humphreys's detailed examination, we learned that the comet was initially observed in China on March 9. The eclipse would have occurred during daylight hours in China, and the comet may not have been visible until the following night. I suggest that it could have been on this particular night just after the birth of Jesus, or in the early morning hours of the following day, that Chinese observers documented the initial sighting of the comet.

After its appearance, the wise men began to follow the comet in order to pay homage to the newborn child in Bethlehem. The stunning appearance of the comet, coming as it did immediately following the eclipse event at 15 degrees Pisces, would have constituted the third and fourth celestial signs that the wise men were seeking in order to begin their long-awaited journey. As we have seen, they could have easily completed a journey to Bethlehem within the seventy days that the comet was visible. This astrological timing fits perfectly with everything we historically know about Herod, the census, the comet, the Great Conjunction, and the wise men's journey.

THE ECLIPSE CHART

Why is a precise moment in time or exact time of birth especially important to astrologers? A vast amount of information can be derived from an accurate horoscope. A solar eclipse is a highly significant astronomical event involving the partial or total obscuring of the sun's light when the body of the moon passes in front of the sun, as seen from Earth. Throughout the ages, an eclipse chart has been shown to provide a huge amount of information regarding the circumstances surrounding relevant human events. The exact timing of a historical eclipse can be made available with computer software and is easily computed today. The time of the eclipse is then placed at the geographical location in question, which in this case is Bethlehem.

It is proposed that Jesus was born during or close to the event of the solar eclipse. We can never really know for certain if the birth occurred at the exact moment of the eclipse. Nevertheless, a horoscope timed to the eclipse can be extraordinarily helpful in identifying many details about his life. In other words, if one is born close enough in time to an eclipse, the eclipse chart itself can be used to signify the birth. To astrologers, a birth that is tied to an eclipse can show an exceedingly intense and exceptional life. For the ancients, an eclipse was known as a sign from God that could portray and magnify a spectacular or highly significant human event.

This is a particularly potent eclipse because it repeats the exact zodiacal degree of the most recent Great Conjunction that occurred in 7 BCE. The repeated degree thus implies an even-greater level of divine power than would normally be associated with an "ordinary" eclipse. Just as we discussed during the birth of King David, the Great Conjunction was used to anticipate the birth of an important king or powerful leader. Here the repeat of the exact same degree as the Great Conjunction can hardly be construed as a random coincidence.

Please see chart 3 for an ancient view of the eclipse chart. We will be using this chart to signify the birth of Christ, particularly since no other birth time can be made available.

NATAL CHART

Mar 8 0005 BC, Wed
7:10:34 am LMT -2:20:48
Bethlehem, Israel
31°N43′ 035°E12′

Geocentric
Tropical
Placidus
True Node

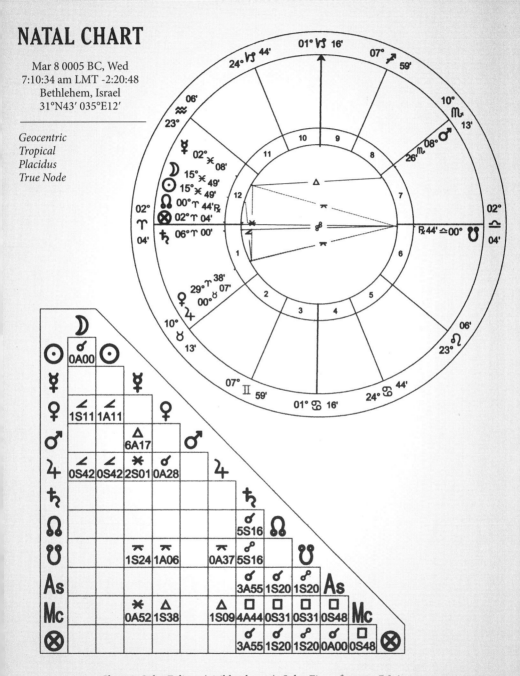

Chart 3: Solar Eclipse (visible planets), _Solar Fire software. v7.0.4_

95

Chart 3 shows the known visible planets, identical to what the wise men would have found in the sky at the exact moment of the eclipse, except that the comet known as the Star of Bethlehem is not shown in the chart. Comets rapidly change position and act as intruders emanating from outside the known solar system. Since they do not conform with a regular orbit around the sun, comets are undetectable by the usual calculation methods used in astrology and solar astronomy to determine planetary movement. For this reason, it is not possible to portray the comet in the horoscope. Nevertheless, from the historical documentation provided by Professor Humphreys, we know the comet would have been visible to the wise men in the night sky, immediately or within a short amount of time following the eclipse.

Chart 4 shows a modern view of the same event, including the more recently discovered planets in the solar system. For the sake of simplicity, I have not included all the optional chart features that are occasionally used by modern astrologers, nor have I included every detail in chart delineation, but I will attempt to describe the highlights of the chart as it pertains to the life and legacy of Jesus Christ.

THE ARIES POINT
AND CRITICAL DEGREES

While at times the following discussion may become unavoidably technical, to assist in understanding by readers who are non-astrologers, any new terminology will be explained as simply as possible. A list of resources is also provided in the appendix for further review by interested parties.

Looking at the eclipse chart, the left side of the horizontal axis indicates 2 Aries on the Ascendant, which is the exact zodiacal point ascending on the eastern horizon at that location in Bethlehem. On the opposite or right side of the horizontal axis, the point known as the Descendant indicates 2 Libra, the point on the ecliptic that was descending at the time of the eclipse.

A second major line in the chart is shown by the vertical axis, located perpendicular to the horizontal axis. The vertical axis indicates 1 Capricorn on the Midheaven or zenith, the highest point overhead at the time of the eclipse. At the bottom of the vertical axis, 1 Cancer is the degree on the Imum Coeli, or lowest point of the chart.

All these major points on the chart axes are located very close to 0 degrees in the cardinal signs. As previously mentioned in an earlier chapter, the zodiacal position at 0 degrees of a cardinal sign is known to astrologers as the Aries Point. Placements within

NATAL CHART

Mar 8 0005 BC, Wed
7:10:34 am LMT -2:20:48
Bethlehem, Israel
31°N43′ 035°E12′

Geocentric
Tropical
Placidus
True Node

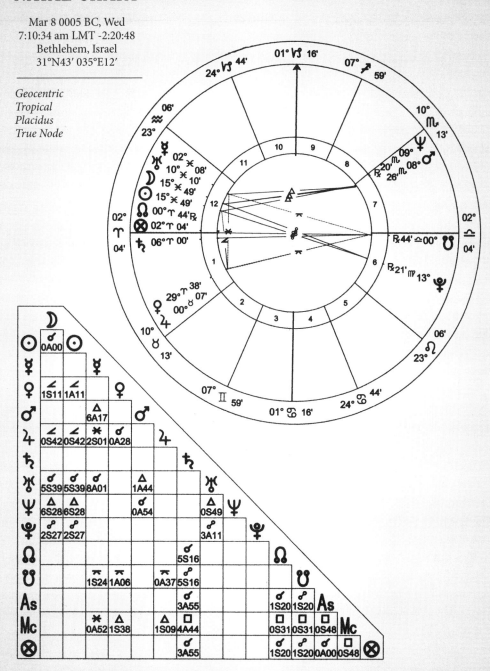

Chart 4: Solar Eclipse (modern planets), using *Solar Fire software. v7.0.4*

2 or 3 degrees of orb (effective degree of range) are recognized as being highly significant.

As you may recall, the Aries Point is considered to be a highly prominent and critical degree that signifies great importance and projection to the rest of the world for whatever is indicated by that particular chart. What makes this effect even more potentially significant is that the nodal axis of the moon is also located at the exact critical degree of the Aries Point. The symbol for the North Node of the moon can be seen above the eastern horizon on the left side of the chart, while the symbol for the South Node of the moon is seen just below the western horizon on the right side of the chart.

The lunar nodes are especially significant to many astrologers as powerful indicators of the life mission. The nodes are determined astronomically by calculating the geometrical intersection of the moon's path as it orbits the Earth and crosses the path of the sun, known as the ecliptic. The two points of intersection, where the plane of the moon's orbit crosses the plane of the ecliptic, form the two nodes of the moon, which are differentiated as the North and South lunar nodes. The lunar nodes are said to indicate the place in the chart where the celestial spirit is brought down to Earth. Clearly, the North Node at exactly 0 degrees in a cardinal sign, and conjoined with the Ascendant on the eastern horizon is an extremely meaningful placement and indicative of a deeply significant event.

In and of themselves, the lunar nodes are considered to be highly sensitive points in the existence of the person or event symbolized by the chart. In addition, any planet or placement square to the nodes (located at a 90-degree angle) is in a position known as the moon's "bendings." The bendings are two additional points that are considered to be highly critical and even "dangerous" (Lehman 1996, 207). Here we find that the chart's Midheaven and Imum Coeli, encompassing the entire vertical axis, both of which are located on Aries Points, are also closely square to the nodes and are therefore located on the moon's bendings.

Why are these zodiacal placements so relevant? Here the placements are *triply* highlighted and magnified. Each placement, in and of itself, is individually considered to be a critical point in the life of the person or event. Yet, these placements in the eclipse chart, including the nodes, the bendings, the axis of the Ascendant, and the axis of the Midheaven, all are located on an Aries Point, and all are closely in conjunction or square to one another. Thus, they are considered to be critical points, found on critical degrees and forming a critical zodiacal relationship with one another.

These critical positions emphasize a highly significant historical event or person born during the time frame represented by the eclipse chart. Severe, crucial, life-changing issues can interrupt or "change the flow of life" for that individual (Lehman 1996, 207). Certainly, the entire life and times of Jesus can hardly be considered as anything but extremely powerful and significant. Life-changing events occurred, both for himself as an individual, and for the rest of the world in terms of religious belief, lasting far beyond the span of his actual physical time on Earth.

HEMISPHERIC EMPHASIS

The North Node in conjunction with the Ascendant coincides with a very strong hemispheric emphasis in the eastern half of the chart. Notice that in addition to the North Node, there are six of the visible planets (and seven of the modern planets) located on the left-hand side of the vertical axis. A chart with many planets crowded on the eastern side of the horoscope indicates an individual with a very strong sense of self, and a determined personal mission in relation to others.

The role of the lunar node conjoined with the Aries Point on the Ascendant intensely describes how the great personal suffering and sacrifice of Jesus Christ became so well known throughout the entire world. Again, the importance of the Aries Point is similar to what we have seen once before, in the conjunction of Mars with the Aries Point in King David's natal chart. However, in this case, the lunar node on the Aries Point brings knowledge of Christ's personal sacrifice to the world at a much-higher level.

The node conjoined with the axis of the Ascendant would significantly intensify the effect of the chart's eastern orientation. The node's exact location on both the Aries Point and the Ascendant, combined with several other factors that will be discussed below, suggests the most powerful level of personal sacrifice that can be imagined. Here we see this intensity in Christ, who for Christians becomes the ultimate savior for all of humanity.

VENUS AND JUPITER

Another significant point in the chart is often the planet affiliated with or dignified by the zodiac sign in which the sun is located; this planet is commonly called one of the "chart rulers" (Lehman 1996; March and McEvers 2008). In this particular horoscope, the sun is located in the sign of Pisces exactly on the degree of the Great Conjunction. The traditional ruler of Pisces is Jupiter; therefore, Jupiter becomes an important planet in delineating the chart.

Astrologers will note that Jupiter is also the "term" ruler (a subdivision ruler) of the degree upon the Ascendant, as well as the "sect" ruler in a day chart. Without going into further detail, suffice it to say that being both a term ruler and a sect ruler adds even more layers of strength and essential planetary dignity, all which are demonstrated here by Jupiter.

It is really quite amazing that Venus and Jupiter are located in exact or nearly exact conjunction. Although they are found in conjoining signs, there is less than 1 zodiacal degree between them. These are the two brightest planets in the solar system, and indeed, other than the moon, they are considered by astronomers as the two brightest objects in the entire night sky. With these two brilliant planets in conjunction at the time of the eclipse, we can imagine the wise men viewing this splendid display in the darkness of the new moon, on a clear night in the desert sky. It would likely be similar in brightness to the comet we call the Star of Bethlehem. The comet would have been seen on one side of the sky in the zodiac sign of Capricorn, while the Venus-Jupiter conjunction was on another side of the sky in late Aries to early Taurus. Everywhere you looked, you would find the brilliant signs from God!

In astrological understanding, the Venus-Jupiter conjunction indicates a markedly high level of enduring affection for others, a sincerely generous spirit, a strong desire to stay on the highest moral ground, and a desire to work so hard to please God. The exaltation of Christ after death can be signified here by the location of these most benefic planets in extremely tight conjunction, forming a close trine aspect (120 degrees) to the Midheaven at the zenith of the chart.

Jupiter also rules the sign of Sagittarius on the ninth-house cusp, where it represents a significant level of religious spirit and intensity (please see the meaning of the ninth house that was previously described in King David's chart). In the traditional system of astrological affinity and zodiacal-sign rulership, Jupiter is considered both the ruler of Sagittarius and the sign Pisces, in which the Great Conjunction occurred.

The location of the Great Conjunction in Pisces and in the twelfth house of the eclipse chart places an even-greater emphasis on Jupiter, as sign ruler and as natural ruler of both the ninth and twelfth houses. This combination represents a supremely elevated level of spiritual connection. Of all the houses in the astrological house system, the twelfth manifests as the highest extent of true spiritual transformation.

In like manner, Venus rules the zodiac sign of Taurus, the sign in which Jupiter is located, and the sign on the second-house cusp, identifying personal values and worldly goods. The combination of these two planets reminds me of the bountiful blessings provided by God, clearly multiplied many times over when Jesus fed huge crowds of people with only a few tiny little fishes. Both Venus and Jupiter in this chart position indicate a true mastery of the most-important values in life, the highest level of mature spiritual understanding, and abundant blessings from God. The appearance of the comet, occurring around the same moment in time as the brilliant Venus-Jupiter conjunction and the eclipse itself, would surely have left no doubt in the minds of the wise men that the celestial signs they had been seeking were finally present.

BORN IN THE SIGN OF WATER

In the eclipse chart, there are four modern planetary bodies (including the moon) located in the sign of Pisces. One of my favorite descriptions of Pisces states the following: "Pisces mirrors like a lake its environment and is moved by every motion near it" (Zain, as found in Doane 1995, 95). This zodiac sign has long been associated with Jesus Christ through his capacity for compassion and deep personal sacrifice, spiritual idealism, a desire for true universal wholeness, and the symbolism of the fishes.

The astrological symbol for Pisces is two fish swimming in opposite directions. Interestingly, the fish symbol has commonly been used by Christians over the millennia to signify their faith. I have often wondered if the early Christians who used this symbolism were aware of the connection between the message of Christ and the zodiac sign of Pisces under which Christ was born.

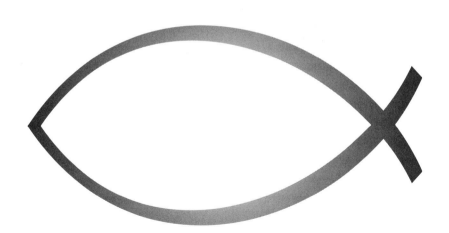

The Ichthus, the sign of the fish

Representing the profile of a fish, the "ichthus" is a symbol consisting of two intersecting arcs. It was used by early Christians as a secret symbol for Christianity when they were undergoing persecution by the Romans. Today we frequently see the same fish symbol proudly displayed on personal automobiles driven by modern Christians. Even the word "ichthus" comes from a combination of Greek letters, which in English translates to mean "Jesus Christ, Son of God, Savior" (Coffman 2008).

The first known use of the fish symbolism in Christian literature was written by an author named Tertullian of Carthage. Born around 160 CE, Tertullian was the first Latin-writing author whose writings are still available today. In his treatise *On Baptism*, a work that supports the practice of baptism with water, Tertullian wrote the following: "We, little fishes, after the example of our ichthus Jesus Christ, are born in water" (Tertullian, as found in Rambo 2010). Here, in the words of one of the earliest known Christian writers, we find an exceptionally direct and astounding statement that tells us the birth of Jesus Christ occurred in the sign of water.

Much of the symbolism of the fish can be found in the gospels. The first disciples of Jesus were fishermen, and Jesus instructed his followers to become *"fishers of men"* (Matthew 4:19). In his third and last appearance to the apostles after the resurrection, Jesus appeared at sea and helped them catch fish. While feeding the apostles the fish they had caught, and using the fish as symbolism, Jesus told his apostles to *"feed my sheep"* (John 21:1–16).

The time being used to symbolize the birth of Christ is the solar eclipse that occurred immediately before or during the birth itself. Being born with an eclipse at the time of birth is an indicator of the strength, emphasis, and intensity of his life. A solar eclipse is a special type of conjunction between the sun and the moon in the astrological chart. As noted earlier, both of these planetary bodies are located in the twelfth-house position, providing a profound emphasis on his keen personal sacrifice for the sake of others. The washing of feet, the role of Christ as nurturer and spiritual guide, and the symbolism of the fish are powerful indicators for this placement in Pisces and the twelfth house.

A conjunction with the sun is also known as a new moon, forming an enormous focus on new beginnings. In this case, the new moon coincides exactly with the Great Conjunction, indicating the birth of a new king for Israel and, indeed, the entire world.

THE INTENSITY OF SATURN

The eclipse chart includes the planet Saturn, located in the sign of Aries, just below the eastern horizon and in the first house. Saturn in this position represents an immense strength of character and self-discipline, an intense personality, a seriousness of purpose, a sound sense of responsibility, powerful personal commitment, and a strong moral solidity. The symbolism provided by Saturn brings to mind the "cornerstone" and the "rock" often described in Christian literature.

However, Saturn is also ruler of the tenth house, which can suggest having an exceptional personal enemy in King Herod. The tenth house traditionally represents authorities and persons who are appointed to positions of power. Another important note about Saturn is that it essentially has no aspects with any of the other planets. Although it is located within orb of conjunction with the lunar node and the axis of the Ascendant, these points are not planets. Aspects with other planets tend to modify the expression of the planet being examined. A planet with no aspects is more acutely powerful and intensified, as the unaspected planet "stands alone" without any modification whatsoever from other planets (Tompkins 2006, 274).

Remember that the Capricorn Midheaven and tenth-house cusp were previously noted to be located on an Aries Point and at the moon's bendings. As ruler of the Midheaven and tenth house, this intensely driven Saturn represents King Herod. Saturn particularly describes Herod's efforts to kill the infant Jesus and other potential rivals, when he decreed that all young children age two and under should be brutally murdered. The resulting acts of intense cruelty and heinous multiple infanticide were recorded throughout history. Among many other actions perpetrated by King Herod, this edict led to his enduring legacy within the flames of infamy.

THE POWER OF MARS

There's more. Astrologers generally consider Mars to be the planet most affiliated with and ruler of the zodiac signs Aries and Scorpio. Aries is located on the Ascendant of the eclipse chart, and Mars is also ruler of the sign in which Saturn is placed. Furthermore, the zodiac sign in which Mars itself is located is its other traditional sign of influence, Scorpio. Thus, great additional force and emphasis can be claimed by Mars, being both the ruler of the Ascendant, and located in the powerful sign of Scorpio.

By house division (representing span of activity), Mars is located in the seventh house of the chart, an angular placement that is related to personal relationships of all kinds, including negative ones. Mars in this position denotes enormous power endowed to the open enemies of Christ, ultimately leading to his eventual trial and crucifixion.

Astrologically, then, we find his enemies to be well represented in the chart through the highly potent combination of Saturn and Mars. As ruler of the Midheaven and tenth house, Saturn represents King Herod and other authority figures. Saturn is intensely located in a strong angular position near the Ascendant. Meanwhile, representing open enemies, Mars is also powerfully located inside the angular seventh house and is found in its own sign of intensity and strength. Both are powerful planets ruling an angle, either the Midheaven or the Ascendant, both are located in strong angular positions, and they tend to work together by virtue of sign rulership and exaltation. Accordingly, Mars is ruler of the sign Aries, the sign in which Saturn is posited, and is exalted in Capricorn, the sign found on the Midheaven of the chart.

Both planets are also traditionally defined as "malefic," meaning they are prone to precipitate problems and difficulties. Found in quite powerful positions, they literally form an archetypal picture of the extremely powerful enemies of Christ.

FINAL DISPOSITOR

There are even more reasons to consider Mars to be an extremely powerful player in the eclipse chart. A planet can stand out by means of being the "final dispositor" of the entire horoscope through the system of astrological sign rulership. It works like this: The sun, moon, and other planets located in Pisces are in a sign ruled by Jupiter. Jupiter, in turn, is located in Taurus, a sign ruled by Venus. Venus is located in Aries (as well as Saturn in Aries), a sign ruled by Mars. Mars itself, located in Scorpio, is in its other sign of rulership and thus has no dispositor behind it. In this stepwise manner, Mars becomes the final dispositor of the entire chart, thereby receiving great additional strength and adding to its malefic tendencies (Tyl 2009).

Astrologers will note that while it is located in the seventh house, Mars is very close to the eighth-house cusp (with an orb of less than 2 degrees). Traditionally known as the "house of death and final transformation," the time of the eclipse places Scorpio on that cusp. To summarize its position, then, Mars is in conjunction with the eighth cusp, ruler of the sign on the eighth house cusp, ruler of the sign on the Ascendant, located in the angular seventh house, placed in a sign of rulership, exalted in the Capricorn Midheaven, and acts as the final dispositor of the eclipse chart.

This exceptionally powerful Mars links all these factors together: the body and person of Christ (Ascendant) being subject to torture and persecution (Saturn) by the Roman and Jewish authorities (Midheaven), who were known to be his personal enemies (seventh house), inevitably leading to his crucifixion, death, and final spiritual transformation (eighth house).

MORE ABOUT CRITICAL DEGREES

To add even more strength to the placement of Mars, there are specific "critical degrees" noteworthy in the eclipse chart. Based on the lunar cycle, a list of critical degrees is a traditional method derived from the moon's average daily motion. In this system, the moon's average daily motion of 12 degrees, 51 minutes, and 25 seconds is added to the beginning of the zodiac at 0 Aries (the Aries Point). By subsequently adding the moon's average daily motion and proceeding around the signs of the zodiac, we arrive at a critical degree located at 8 degrees 34 minutes of Scorpio.

In this case using only very small orbs, astrologers consider the lunar critical degrees to be points of heightened sensitivity, and interpret these points to give additional emphasis to any planet located on that specific degree (March and McEvers 2009). Here in the eclipse chart, adding to all the other emphases already noted, Mars is located at 8 degrees of Scorpio, precisely on a lunar degree.

One additional critical degree is worth mentioning. The final degree of a sign, starting at 29 degrees 0 minutes and ending at 29 degrees 59 minutes, is known as the "anaretic degree." Astrologically, the final degree represents a sense of "inevitability, irrevocability, and finality—the end of a familiar path . . . a lifelong mission to resolve and come to terms with these issues which we seem to have been saddled with at birth," and a "knowingness" of the inevitable nature of the life course (Clifford n.d.).

With Venus at 29 Aries in the chart, we see this sense of the inevitable regarding the body and personal life of Christ (Venus is located in the first house), his personal values (Venus is ruler of the sign on the second-house cusp), and with regard to his personal enemies (Venus is also ruler of the sign on the seventh-house cusp).

CONSIDERING PLUTO

Some other thoughts regarding the eclipse chart concern the placement of the modern planet Pluto (as seen in chart 4). Found in the sign of Virgo, Pluto is located in the sixth house and forms a close opposition aspect (180 degrees) with the sun and moon in the twelfth house. In the natural alignment of the zodiac, the sixth house corresponds to the concept of service, while the twelfth house characterizes the condition of self-sacrifice.

The sun-Pluto opposition is an indicator for severe personal trauma, crisis, and subsequent transformation, corroborating many of the other chart factors already mentioned. We should also remember that all the innocent young victims murdered by Herod were born around the same time period in the vicinity of Bethlehem. These children were born, lived a very short life, and died under the influence of the same eclipse.

In a personal chart, emphasis on Pisces and the twelfth house places an extraordinary orientation on great inner strength, intuitive capability, power of the subconscious, and a need for self-sacrifice for the sake of others. The addition of the opposition aspect provides an overwhelming awareness and acceptance of that orientation and purpose. Christ often found it necessary to seek places of seclusion and solitude for quiet reflection and prayer. The enormous intensity and force of his inner life with God can thus be seen through the positions of the sun and moon in the twelfth house and found in opposition to Pluto.

THE PART OF FORTUNE

One other chart feature that seems to be highly relevant in the eclipse chart is known as the "Part of Fortune." Ancient astrologers gave special attention and prominence to this point, which is mathematically derived from the zodiacal degrees of the Ascendant, sun, and moon.

The Part of Fortune is represented by a glyph that features a cross within a circle (the axes signify where the Earth and sky are joined together within the celestial sphere). This point suggests the location on Earth where spirit and body uniquely join together. The Part of Fortune traditionally symbolizes the expression of the vital life force divinely descending down onto the plane of the Earth, and where the life purpose can be expressed and flow most easily (George 2008).

In Bethlehem at the time of the eclipse, the Part of Fortune is located very close to the Aries Point and exactly on the horizon. By definition, the Part of Fortune will always be on the Ascendant during an eclipse, but being in close proximity to the Aries Point is extremely uncommon, reflecting God's special plan for the birth of Christ. As the Aries Point seems to multiply the effects of anything that touches it, so the world has become intensely aware of the events surrounding the birth of Christ.

SO JUST WHAT HAPPENED HERE?

Upon viewing the eclipse, the wise men, learned in astrology, would surely have realized they were witnessing a truly significant event. To the wise men, the physical manifestation of the eclipse, portrayed in the starry map of the sky, represents God's will in a format they could actually read and understand. This particular eclipse chart is dramatically unique in that it includes a huge and unprecedented number of critical points. It virtually shouts at everyone to stand up and pay attention!

To clearly illustrate this point, let us summarize the critical points. There are nine positions on or very close to the Aries Point: the four chart angles (the Ascendant and Midheaven, along with their corresponding opposite angles), the two nodes of the moon, the two bendings of the moon, and the Part of Fortune. There is one planet located on a lunar critical degree, Mars, which is the highly powerful final dispositor of the chart. There is another planet, Venus, located on an anaretic degree.

The total comes to eleven critical-degree positions featured in the eclipse chart, a number that is truly exceptional. Finding even a total of four positions on critical degrees in a chart is relatively rare and can be deemed an unusual event. Thus, the number of critical degrees found here in the eclipse chart seems absolutely unprecedented.

The final message is clear: God is real. The story of Jesus Christ is real. And the manifestation of God's will is real. The incontrovertible evidence can be found written in the map of the eclipse chart, for any astrologer or person who has the ability and understanding to read it. Those who have achieved this level of understanding are truly wise and must surely celebrate: for the physical manifestation inscribed into the sky represents the enduring proof of God's will, cast into the heavens and available for those of us who are willing to see and understand.

Chapter X
THE CHRISTIAN DILEMMA

Today, Christianity has many forms, divisions, denominations, and traditions. But in all its many forms, Christianity holds a few core beliefs. The first core belief is that Jesus Christ is savior, and through his sacrifice on the cross, acceptance of Christ becomes the path to salvation, a personal relationship with God, and everlasting life. These beliefs and doctrines are written in the New Testament of the Bible.

We provided evidence that astrology formed a fundamental structure behind many ancient Jewish customs and traditions, clearly seen within the writings of the Old Testament as well as other physical proof. We determined that astrology performed an unmistakable and indispensable role in the belief system held by ancestors of the Jewish people. And we demonstrated that this belief system was subsequently passed down to the early followers of Christ, many of whom were themselves Jewish.

Consistent with Jewish tradition, a second core belief of Christianity considers the Ten Commandments to be an essential moral code of behavior for human beings. This code was laid out in the Old Testament of the Bible and is still being followed by Christians today.

A third core belief of Christianity is an understanding that the Holy Bible is God's true word. Nowhere in the Bible is there a condemnation of astrology. Through extensive confirmation of text within both the Old and New Testaments, we know that the worldview demonstrated by astrology was shared by early Christians. We looked at numerous quotations from the Bible supporting both astrology and a worldview that endeavors to see the world and everything in it as a creation of God. Thus, all the celestial spheres, the lights of the sun and moon, the planets, the stars, and everything else in the heavens above correspond to a divine order ordained by God. The entire cosmos, particularly including all the celestial signs that directly pertain to human affairs, was created by God and corresponds to God's grand design.

As a result, we demonstrated that an ordained celestial design including astrology is clearly described and supported by the Bible. Anyone reading and believing in the Bible must come to this same basic conclusion. Yet, there is an unfortunate dilemma in which Christians find themselves today. Dating back to the time of St. Augustine in the fourth and fifth centuries CE, certain patriarchs of the Roman Catholic Church have condemned astrology and, to this day, continue to do so. In this chapter, we shall explore some of the factors related to this wrongful ideological position. While often repeated, any condemnation by the Roman church is not truly relevant toward the inherently meaningful association between astrology and Christian belief.

It cannot be denied that the horoscope is a map of the heavens, which were formed under the direction and creation of God. The study of astrology allows us to expand our mundane worldview and see more directly the blessings that are sent to us from God. Like Isaiah, Samuel, David, Daniel, and the wise men, we are seeking signs from the heavens in order to assist our understanding of God's will for our lives here on Earth. Astrology becomes the manner in which divine celestial and astronomical events are significantly linked to human affairs. The close, meaningful, and enduring correspondence between God's will and human events clearly goes to the heart of the study of astrology.

THE WORKS AND WORDS OF JESUS

Many times in the scriptures, when speaking in parables to the apostles, Jesus regularly repeated the number 7. Just as we have seen in the Old Testament, this number represents the seven visible planets. Jesus also frequently repeated the number 12, the number representing the twelve astrological signs of the zodiac. No other numbers were chosen more often. He even chose twelve apostles: *"And when he had called upon him his twelve apostles, he gave them power against unclean spirits, to cast them out, and to heal all manner of sickness and all manner of disease"* (Matthew 10:1).

Upon feeding a multitude of 5,000, Jesus miraculously divided five loaves of bread and two fishes (from an original total of seven items), until there were twelve baskets of food remaining (Matthew 14:19–20; Mark 6:41–44). At another time, Jesus blessed seven loaves of bread that were used to feed a multitude of 4,000, and seven full baskets of food remained (Matthew 15:33–37; Mark 8:5–8).

Indeed, Jesus made sure that his apostles paid close attention and fully understood the special meaning of these numbers, since he later admonished them for their lack of understanding:

> Having eyes, see ye not? and having ears, hear ye not? and do ye not remember? When I brake the five loaves among the five thousand, how many baskets full of fragments took ye up? They say unto him, Twelve. And when the seven among four thousand, how many baskets full of fragments took ye up? And they say, Seven. And he said unto them, How is it that ye do not understand? (Mark 8:18–21).

Here we should remember that astrology was an unquestionably integral part of Jewish culture and the surrounding Roman Empire. Jesus was clearly speaking of astronomical signs when he foretold of the forthcoming destruction of Jerusalem in Luke 21. This information obviously upset the apostles, who would have had family in the area and would certainly have worshiped at the temple in Jerusalem. Jesus stated:

> Great signs shall there be from heaven. . . . And there shall be signs in the sun, and in the moon, and in the stars. . . . And then shall they see the Son of man coming in a cloud with great power and great glory. And when these things begin to come to pass, then look up, and lift your heads; for your redemption draweth nigh (Luke 21:11, 25, 27–28).

Yet Jesus refused to provide any signs to the Pharisees, because they were unworthy to receive a sign from God: "A wicked and adulterous generation seeketh after a sign; and there shall be no sign given unto it, but the sign of the prophet Jonas. And he left them, and departed" (Matthew 16:4). Consequently, when the Pharisees tempted Jesus to provide a sign from heaven, he refused, and furthermore, he charged the apostles: "Take heed, beware of the leaven of the Pharisees, and of the leaven of Herod" (Mark 15:15).

In this way, as Jesus warned the apostles, we learn that the wicked and the evil shall not be deemed appropriate to receive the celestial signs ordained by God. Just as Jesus so clearly proclaimed, only those among the righteous shall receive a sign from God.

HOROSCOPES AS CELESTIAL SIGNS

Very few individuals will receive such special astrological significance as found in the horoscopes that were introduced for David and the eclipse chart representing the birth of Jesus. When considering the charts for David and the eclipse, keep in mind the importance of the Aries Point. A strong emphasis on the Aries Point often indicates the rare individuals who will change the course of history forever, long after their own bodily lives have ended in physical death. Yet for each of us as individuals, beginning with birth, each person will nevertheless receive a unique astrological pattern that was given to us by God. Learning to address those chart patterns will allow us to identify and accept what is most difficult in our lives, as well as to make better use of what is most beneficial in our lives.

Given the widespread use of astrology around the time of Christ's nativity, it is highly probable that the birth date and horoscope for Jesus Christ became known to early Christian investigators, particularly because of the Great Conjunction occurring prior to his birth. Nevertheless, it is my suspicion that authorities in the early Roman church decided to obscure this vital information. The reasons for doing so can never be truly known, but it is possible that early church leaders may have viewed Christ's natal chart as "weak," essentially for the following reasons.

First, the natal sun and moon are located in the sign of Pisces. Second, emphasis is placed on these bodies and other important points in the twelfth-house division of the chart. Typically, both Pisces and the twelfth house were seen as cadent or weaker positions due to their traditional astrological connection with sacrifice, servitude, slaves, prisons, places of seclusion, the realm of the unconscious, and spiritual service for the sake of others.

Third, very few planets are located in cardinal-sign placements within the horoscope. Traditional astrologers noticed that planets placed in cardinal signs generally manifest with much greater urgency, strength, and authority, in a manner that can be easily and directly observed. But the eclipse horoscope used to represent the birth of Christ contains only two planets placed in cardinal signs. One of these planets is Saturn, and as previously discussed, most meaningfully describes the enormous strength and malevolent power of the enemies of Christ.

In many human lives, depending on the planetary placements, dignities, aspects, and other important chart factors, cardinal energy can be expressed in a very positive manner and often indicates intensity, action, ardor, ambition, initiative, and enthusiasm. But when used inappropriately, the cardinal quality can become overly ambitious, autocratic, inconsiderate, hasty, difficult, and domineering. We can see how these latter qualities especially describe the enemies of Christ.

The predominance of planets in both Pisces and the twelfth-house positions in the eclipse chart pertain, in astrological terms, to a mutable quality and a cadent orientation. To astrologers, both these terms commonly emphasize a keen perception, a great versatility, a willingness to adapt, an elevated sympathy for others, an orientation to serve, and an extraordinarily high level of intuition. Like the reed that bends in the storm, the mutable personality often weathers the storm much better than the mighty but fixated oak, which tends to split in half when heavy storm winds blow.

Accordingly, the predominance of mutable and cadent planetary positions in a horoscope can be viewed as providing that person with greater internal sympathy. There is a tendency to be introspective and motivated internally rather than externally. Persons with this orientation tend to have a greater focus on religious belief, a deeper understanding of the subconscious, and a hidden (rather than overt) compassion and inner strength.

Nevertheless, it is quite plausible to conjecture that having the leader of the Christian religion viewed in the manner of a Pisces, cadent, mutable orientation may have led to the decision by early fathers of the Roman church to keep the information on his nativity secret. Traditional kings and conventional leaders were presumed to accentuate the cardinal personality, highlighting tremendous ambition, action, and initiative. It is noteworthy that from an early age, higher-level church bishops adopted the title of "Cardinals" in order to exalt themselves and their role. Clearly, Christ was not ambitious to promote himself over others; he maintained a role of self-denial, allowed brutal actions by enemies and other people to lead to his own personal sacrifice, and refused to save himself from suffering on the cross.

Ironically, even the likelihood of the scenario described above, whereby church leaders would deliberately obscure factual evidence surrounding the nativity of Christ, can be identified in the modern eclipse chart for Christ. The planet Pluto is located in the sixth house and in the sign of Virgo, forming a direct opposition to the position of the eclipse. This location of Pluto can describe hidden intent, the potential power and over-ambition of authorities behind the scenes, deliberate subterfuge, martyrdom, and the destruction of important details.

In contrast to what must remain as only a theoretical reaction by church authorities, however, it is my view that the positions of natal planets in Pisces, as well as the cadent-house emphasis, are deeply reflective of the true reality of Christ. These planetary positions signify a sincere level of spiritual service to humanity as his life purpose, leading to his final achievement, the sacrifice and final transcendence of Christ. His role as savior, with his legacy of unsurpassed personal suffering and profound individual sacrifice for the needs of the collective, could hardly be better expressed than in the eclipse chart.

AN UNJUST CONDEMNATION OF ASTROLOGY

To this day, the Catechism of the Roman Catholic Church continues to unjustly condemn astrology as a form of conciliation to demonic powers (Campion 2012). In response, we should remind church authorities that the profound intrinsic correspondence between heaven and Earth was created by God and is unquestionably supported by writings in the Bible. As written in the scriptures, the heavens were specifically designed by God to assist in human understanding of God's will through the study of celestial events. It is illogical to deny either God's hand in this process, or astrology's place in the grand scheme created by God.

In this regard, a noted historical researcher succinctly writes:

> The point is that the condemnation of astrology represented only the position of a small group of theologians who were involved in a perpetual power struggle for control of official doctrine. After 312 they were backed by the emperors, for whom theological centralism was seen as essential to the effort to retain control of a disintegrating empire (Campion 2008, 286).

By the end of the fourth century CE, the Roman Empire was thrown into a state of civil war, constant political crisis involving rival generals, and the peril of threatening invasions. Closely within this time frame, the great city of Rome was sacked by invading barbarians in the year 410.

We also know that St. Augustine was born toward the end of the Roman Empire, during the fourth century CE. Most astrologers during that time period did not offer sacrifices and did not worship demons, planets, or idolatrous spirits during the practice of astrology. Many astrologers of that time period were Christians. Yet, it is possible that during the life time of Augustine, idolatry was still being practiced by a small number of pagan or Babylonian-type astrologers who continued to live within the community. Nevertheless, Augustine erroneously but deliberately lumped all astrologers into this small group.

It appears that Augustine fundamentally objected to astrology because astrology "introduced a dangerous and democratic element which had to be stamped out. He was concerned both to crush pagan astrology and to head off a rise of a Christian astrology, which he clearly saw as a potential threat" to the authority of the newly emerging Roman church (Campion 2008, 281). Augustine may or may not have been aware of the natural celestial influence portrayed by astrology, and the link between life on Earth and the movements of the planetary bodies. But evidently, the writings of Augustine in condemning astrology were based, more than anything, upon a political strategy rather than for theological reasons. His writings are far-reaching and are accepted today without any further discussion by many modern church authorities.

The combination of this political strategy, along with certain ongoing cultural factors, eventually led to the decline of astrology throughout western Europe. As war and invasion from competing tribes in the region rapidly increased, a sharp decrease in literacy took place. In particular, a decrease in knowledge of the Greek language occurred; Greek was the predominant language in which many books of that era, including the New Testament, were written.

With the ongoing risk of invasion, an extensive disintegration of Roman culture quickly ensued. Along with actual intrusions from invading northern armies and Germanic tribes, a state of collective fear existed in Rome during the life of Augustine. These greatly disruptive events generated a deep political expediency to consolidate Christian theology. By disposing of astrology and other competing Christian theologies, Augustine adroitly led the theological consolidation of the Christian religion. From this point onward, Christianity diverged from the many diverse competing theologies, which included Christian astrology, into only one particular theology that was explicitly approved by the Roman Catholic Church (Campion 2008).

THE ASTROLOGICAL HERITAGE

To summarize, a great many statements in the Bible confirm the importance and acceptance of astrology during the time of the ancient Hebrew people, and within the cultures surrounding the writing of the Old and New Testaments. In the centuries preceding the birth of Christ, astrology had flourished and developed under the teachings of Plato and during the Greek Hellenistic period. But by the fourth century CE and beyond, cultural forces derived primarily from political motivations led to the condemnation of astrology by St. Augustine and prevailing Roman church authorities. At this point, astrology was then pushed into a lengthy decline in Western culture.

Obviously, many of those previous political motivations are not acceptable or justified today. It is hoped that the current philosophical thinking of Roman church authorities can advance beyond the old politics, can acknowledge modern ideas, and can be open to valid theological viewpoints other than their own. If astrology is not valid, then it would be statistically impossible for the astounding number of coincidental relationships between horoscope charts and the existing historical facts to be considered mere random chance. Let us briefly summarize some of the findings from the charts that were examined.

In King David's chart, we found the exact Great Conjunction of Jupiter and Saturn, the characteristically defining series of grand trines, a deeply corresponding sign and house emphasis, and an exalted Mars exactly conjoined with the Aries Point, all closely fitting every historical description of his life.

In the solar eclipse chart representing the birth of Christ, we determined that the eclipse repeated the exact and distinct degree of another important Great Conjunction prior to his birth. The chart axes, lunar nodes, moon's bendings, and Part of Fortune (indicating the celestial spirit brought down to Earth) were all located on an Aries Point. We discovered an intensely accurate description of Christ and his life purpose in the Pisces planetary positions and the corresponding twelfth-house emphasis. An angular and strong cardinal Saturn described the intensity of his life; this intense Saturn and a forcefully strong Mars combined to represent the enemies of Christ. Together, the combination of the eclipse at the exact degree of the Great Conjunction, the brilliant Venus-Jupiter conjunction, and the corresponding Star of Bethlehem comet phenomenon produced the celestial signs being sought by the wise men.

THE MODERN DILEMMA

Yet the Christian dilemma remains. How can faithful Christians, particularly Roman Catholics, reconcile the traditional anti-astrology platform of the Roman Catholic Church, in light of the insights provided by God's word, as found in the scriptures, that pertain to the use of astrology? Let us review these fundamental issues.

ONE: God's written word, as shown in the Holy Bible, provides the basis for our knowledge of a divine celestial design created by God. In numerous passages, scriptures from the Bible clearly indicate that a primary purpose of this divine celestial order is to provide signs from heaven. As written in Genesis and elsewhere in the Bible, God intended the celestial signs to be used by humanity in order to help us understand God's will.

TWO: The practice of astrology demonstrates that a divine celestial order was created by God. Astrology records a close correspondence between the movements of the planets with human nativities and activities and confirms that the correspondence of celestial events to God's will actually exists.

THREE: The practice of astrology also confirms that the planets and stars do not cause or "make" anything happen. Correspondence does not imply cause. Each person individually has the choice whether or not to follow the will of God. Astrology allows individuals to identify more profoundly with their own basic characteristics, individual desires, personal relationships, and potential conflicts, but astrology always allows personal free choice, never forces action, and is not deterministic in nature.

FOUR: Nevertheless, for whatever political or historical reasons were used at the time, astrology was erroneously condemned by early Roman church authorities. For almost two thousand years, this erroneous and unjustified condemnation of astrology was brought down through the ages, has never changed, and henceforth remains a major stumbling block for many Christians today who do not wish to question church authority.

At this point in the discussion, every person must make a decision. Do you follow the writings and scriptures found in the Bible, which have been proven to endorse and actually demonstrate astrology? Or do you follow the orders initiated by ancient church authorities following St. Augustine, who originally condemned astrology, not for theological reasons, but clearly for historical and political purposes of their own? The Roman Catholic Church has found it convenient to carry the patently illogical and incorrect condemnation of astrology down through the centuries, but certainly the longevity or age of this condemnation does not improve its validity. I believe you already know what my decision has been in this matter. What personal decision will you make?

Chapter XI:
PUTTING ASTROLOGY INTO PRACTICE

It is not the purpose of this book to provide full instructions for constructing and interpreting astrological charts, but it may be helpful for readers to understand some of the basic ideas and philosophy of astrology in order to effectively manage personal information found in their natal horoscopes. Each birth chart is unique and requires careful examination and specific interpretation based on the individual's life circumstances. The cyclic nature of planetary movements can be seen when viewing birth charts across the different generations, and it is important to remember that the planets move constantly through space over any given period of time.

Interpretation of the birth chart is so much more involved than the sun-sign astrology often found in newspaper columns and magazines. A case could be made that the popular sun-sign columns have done more harm than good to the public perception of astrology. Astrology involves a thorough study and understanding of all the planetary positions, interactions, and movements, not just that of the sun. Knowledge of the Ascendant, or the sign rising on the horizon at the time of birth, will change the interpretation of any transit immensely.

All too often, we repeatedly hear people asking the following questions when faced with rather difficult life situations: "Oh why me, Lord? Oh, why is this happening to me?" Perhaps you, too, sometimes wonder why certain events are happening specifically to you, but not to other people. Maybe you wonder why you must undergo a particularly demanding life circumstance. Perhaps you want to know why your neighbor seems to have all the good luck, and meanwhile, you have nothing but bad luck. The answers to these questions and many more can be found embedded within the birth chart.

But first, let's set our priorities straight. The horoscope or birth chart is not meant to force you, coerce you, hurt you, or replace prayer and a relationship with God. It is only meant to be a guide, a sign, or a tool to help you understand your life path. You always have personal control over your attitude, your decisions, and the choices that you make throughout life. In addition, no single birth chart is better or worse than any other, just different. Personal life circumstances are not always what they might appear to be on the surface.

Selected Astrological Chart Concepts:
THE MODALITIES

When viewing the birth chart, a discussion of the concept of "modality" is helpful in understanding some of the basic differences in human nature. The twelve signs of the zodiac are divided into three main modalities that indicate certain modes or qualities of behavior. Each modality demonstrates a "distinct mode of operating in life" (March and McEvers 2008).

The cardinal modality corresponds to the four changing seasons and the four cardinal points of the compass, which are east, west, north, and south. The cardinal modality is predominant in a personality when there are many planets placed in the cardinal signs (Aries, Cancer, Libra, and Capricorn) or placed in angular house positions.

Remember that an angular house position is a location next to an axis or angle of the chart. In turn, the axes and angles of a chart are determined by their location on the ecliptic at the time of birth. Corresponding to the changing seasons, the predominantly cardinal personality creates a focus on change, initiative, action, ambition, and independence and represents an outgoing, ardent, or enthusiastic individual. On the negative side, the cardinal personality may be overly ambitious, domineering, and unable to finish projects that he has started.

The fixed modality corresponds to many planets found in the fixed signs (Taurus, Leo, Scorpio, and Aquarius) or located in the succedent houses (the second or middle house groupings in relation to the angles) of the horoscope. The predominantly fixed personality is practical, stable, resolute, acquisitive, and dependable and may not be easily swayed by the opinions of others. He is likely to be determined and dignified and can have great power of concentration, but potentially the fixed-modality personality may also become entrenched, unwilling to change, overly set in his ways, and slow to take action.

The mutable modality corresponds to many planets located in the mutable signs (Gemini, Virgo, Sagittarius, and Pisces) or located in cadent positions (the third or last house groupings in relation to the angles) in the horoscope. The predominantly mutable personality is sympathetic, flexible, versatile, and thoughtful and is capable of great religious visualizations. The mutable personality is receptive and reactive but may often allow other people to take the lead, and may allow activities to happen to him, rather than be initiated by him. He is likely to be more internally motivated, deeply intuitive, philosophical, and concerned with the profound meanings in life. On the negative side, the mutable personality may sometimes become deceptive and undependable and lack constancy.

Knowledge of the three fundamental modalities helps us understand some of the basic human differences between people. Every individual is always a blend of the three main modalities. However, one modality will often stand out or will be expressed more frequently in that person's behavior patterns. An even balance of the three modalities will often indicate a well-rounded individual.

THE ASTROLOGICAL HOUSES

The individual placement of planets by house position in the natal chart is another very important consideration. The houses are twelve basic divisions or sections of the horoscope that indicate specific human activities and functions. The house cusps mark the house divisions and change according to the exact time and place of birth, as the constant rotation of the Earth causes the ascending sign and degree to vary. This constant variation determines where the zodiac signs are placed on the natal chart wheel, and then produces the different house positions. Thus, depending on the time and location at birth, the house positions will be different for everyone, making no two birth charts completely identical.

A review of the planetary-house positions can indicate the functions or areas of life that are of greatest potential concern to an individual. In astrology, each celestial house has a meaning or field of activity. As seen in the life of David, the position of several planets in the ninth house represents an enormous emphasis on religious understanding and consequence, along with the essential importance of prayer and his being right with God. As seen in the life of Christ, the position of several planets in the twelfth house of the eclipse chart indicates his overwhelming concern with personal sacrifice for the sake of others, religious visualization, and the renewal of life after death. In addition, we saw that the placement of Mars in the seventh house represents a forceful and powerful enemy or adversary.

We all know of certain individuals who spend the majority of their lives in the pursuit of honor, achievement, and profession. Another individual may be more concerned with money, investments, debts, and the accumulation of wealth or possessions. A third individual may be mainly concerned with personal relationships, marriage, children, the home, and family. A fourth individual may follow a life of quiet reflection, philosophy, religion, or teaching. In all these examples, the house positions can be used to discern the predominant concern, career, or activity found within the individual birth chart. Individuals will have certain house positions in their birth charts consistent with their chosen or predominant life activity.

PLANETS AND ASPECTS

Another important chart factor is the location of planets such as Saturn in the natal horoscope. The placement of Saturn at birth will often indicate in what area of life the individual needs to work hard or tends to have frustrations and conflict. Every year as Saturn travels on its continuous journey through the signs of the zodiac, the changing placement of Saturn as it transits though the different houses of the natal horoscope can indicate a new area of life where problems are prone to crop up.

Alternatively, the more promising planetary positions, such as Venus and Jupiter, can indicate areas of talent, ease, prosperity, and even the propensity for good luck in the life of the individual. As these planets transit through the houses of the birth chart, they often bring a promise for success and benefits to whatever area of life that particular house represents.

Each of the ten basic planetary positions (including the luminaries) assumes its own intrinsic meaning wherever it is found within the birth chart. The study of astrology intricately blends the basic meaning of each planet within the zodiac sign in which it is placed, then incorporates that meaning into the house in which it is located, and determines the energy flow of the planet through a study of the planetary aspects.

We learned that the planetary aspects are the geometrical patterns, which are formed between the planets and the angles of the chart. These aspects and chart patterns can indicate whether the flow of energy among the various chart factors will prove to be more harmonious or more challenging for each individual. The overall mix of the natal locations by zodiac sign, house placement, and aspect patterns, as well as the changing planetary locations by ongoing transit, provides a tremendous amount of information that can be tapped by the astrologer when counseling the individual.

AN INDIVIDUAL PATH

It is critical to remember that the horoscope is our way of viewing God's design for the individual. Knowledge of the horoscope can allow us a deeper understanding of our life purpose; why we were put here on Earth; the difficulties, talents, and focus we have in this life; and how to follow God's individual path for each one of us. We are never forced or coerced by the horoscope to do anything, but it can be used to help us understand a true life path. If we tend to follow a course that differs from what God has chosen for us, we will most likely become unhappy, miserable, and desperate. But if we can understand and realize the track chosen for us by God, we can usually find greater meaning, acceptance, and happiness in life.

Not every person will achieve his or her life goals. The goals themselves are deeply personal and should be different for everyone. But through the practice of astrology, we can reach an understanding of these basic differences between people and realize that different life paths require different means of action. What is appropriate for one person is not necessarily appropriate for another. Through astrology, you can learn about yourself, your predominant modality, the predominant house emphasis or focus in your life, your own personal talents, and a description of the areas of life most prone to incur challenges or problems.

Once we realize that we are supposed to be this way, that God made us this way for a purpose, only then can we begin to actually develop that purpose. Would you rather be left floundering around in the dark and wandering about without any knowledge of the overall design for your life? Or would you rather have a clear idea of your path and a greater understanding of how to reach your personal goals? The study of astrology can help provide a detailed map of that path that personally exists within every one of us.

Putting similar ideas into words, Steven Forrest eloquently describes his thoughts on the study of astrology:

> We're born, and from that moment we carry inside ourselves a little hologram of the sky. As long as we live, it resonates with the rhythms of the planets and tides, stars and seasons. That hologram is our life; its breath is the breathing of an intelligent, conscious universe. Studying that hologram is the delicate, ever-changing art we call astrology (Forrest 1993, 8).

AN IMPORTANT NOTE TO ASTROLOGERS

In the far olden days of pagan astrology, there were undoubtedly many astrologers who originally came from cultural backgrounds and traditions other than Judaism. Before the acceptance of monotheism in the Western world, these astrologers often referred to the planets as "gods" and "goddesses." Either the old pagan gods were named after the planets, or the planets themselves were named after the old gods; it really doesn't matter which came first. Nevertheless, in the modern world today, there are still a few traditional astrologers who routinely refer to the planets and other planetary bodies, such as asteroids, as gods and goddesses. To those astrologers, I would ask you to immediately stop this practice. In today's world, that terminology is incorrect.

Unless you are a true pagan and actually believe in a system of multiple gods and goddesses, you are giving the wrong impression to the rest of the world. When you use such terminology and refer to the planets as gods, you deny a belief in a monotheistic God, and you deny a belief in Christianity. Clearly you are sending the wrong message to all who are watching, and you are certifying that the writings of St. Augustine against pagan astrology still maintain value in today's world.

It is my understanding that many who are guilty of this practice do not truly worship multiple gods but are simply trying to emulate or write in the manner of a few ancient astrologers who actually did practice idolatry. When you use the terminology of gods and goddesses, beware that you are literally turning people off to the study of astrology. There is no place in modern astrology for the practice of idolatry, the worship of multiple gods, or even the slightest impression of such behavior. Anything giving the impression of that type of worship should be strictly avoided.

A FINAL WORD FOR CHRISTIANS

Far too often, as a member of a Christian church, I have sat in the congregation or Sunday school class and silently listened as a priest, preacher, minister, or Sunday school teacher railed on and on about the "evils" of astrology. Perhaps their derogatory statements were based, at least in part, on the inept use of language or inappropriate terminology used by some astrologers, as mentioned above. Nonetheless, I will no longer be silent. Clearly, negative misstatements about astrology are based not on factual evidence from the Bible, but solely upon untruths and innuendo that continue to be passed along from one misinformed person to another. Please refer to the biblical passages cited in this book in support of God's celestial plan that includes astrology.

Many ministers refer to biblical passages telling us to avoid "false prophets." That is excellent advice for everyone but does not explicitly apply to astrologers. As previous sections of this book have amply demonstrated, the wise men and astrologers of the Bible were true men of wisdom, understanding, and spirit. They worshiped God, were blessed by God, and included men such as Samuel and Daniel.

There are only very few instances in the Bible where astrologers are specifically denounced or chastised. In contrast, we have cited a great many scriptures that support astrology and the wise men. Yet, opponents of astrology often quote only one specific passage found in Isaiah that prophesizes the destruction of Babylon. Let us look more closely at this passage.

When read in context, we notice there are several previous passages throughout the book of Isaiah that denounce both Israel and Babylon for their worship of idols and false gods. Because the Babylonians often used astrologers as counselors, Isaiah states that even the astrologers cannot save Babylon from the destruction he has foretold. Speaking to Babylon, Isaiah says:

> Stand now with thine enchantments, and with the multitude of thy sorceries, wherein thou hast labored from thy youth; if so be, thou shalt be able to profit, if so be, thou mayest prevail. Thou art wearied in the multitude of thy counsels. Let now the astrologers, the stargazers, the monthly prognosticators, stand up and save thee from these things that shall come upon thee. Behold, they shall be as stubble; the fire shall burn them; they shall not deliver themselves from the power of the flame: there shall not be a coal to warm at, nor fire to sit before it. Thus shall they be unto thee with whom thou hast laboured, even thy merchants, from thy youth: they shall wander every one to his quarter; none shall save thee (Isaiah 47:12–15).

These passages do not denounce astrology in and of itself for any other reason, except to say that counsel from astrologers cannot be used to save Babylon from Isaiah's prophecy. Earlier passages in Isaiah make it clear that due to the practice of idolatry, the destruction of Babylon is assured. Here Isaiah states that even the astrologers will not be able to save Babylon from final destruction. There is no denunciation of astrology indicated in these passages, only that the astrologers and everyone else who has labored to assist Babylon will be also included in its conflagration. Isaiah says, *"even thy merchants"* will be swept into the flame, and *"none shall save thee."* Does Isaiah's statement here suggest that every merchant must be evil? Surely not!

In denouncing Babylon, Isaiah makes no derogatory statements whatsoever against the actual principles and practices of astrology itself. In other sections of the same book, Isaiah remarks that the great span of sky and the entire host of the heavens are under God's will and command (Isaiah 40:10–12, 45:12). Isaiah goes on to tell us that God called all of the stars by name (Isaiah 40:26), and elsewhere we learned that the *"stars in their courses"* assisted Israel during times of war (Judges 5:20). Indeed, we found many biblical references identifying Daniel and the wise men as astrologers, and we reviewed scriptural evidence describing the goodly pursuit of wisdom and knowledge through the study of the stars.

Moreover, astrologers were clearly not included in any of the groups warned against in the Bible. Explicit warnings were mentioned against false prophets, shamans, witchcraft, warlocks, whoremongers, idolaters, and other such groups. But never were astrologers implicated in any of these lists. Always remember that astrologers were identified as the wise men of the Bible! Today, astrologers are known to view and study the universe with great reverence, wonder, and amazement, and astrologers have the unique ability to see God's creations profoundly at work in human lives, in a deeply personal way.

Whether or not you practice astrology yourself, it is important to always keep an open mind about why astrology works. No one who has truly studied astrology has denied its value or worth. Only those individuals who know nothing about astrology have declared astrology to be meaningless. Be aware that the superficial "sun-sign" astrology (as commonly found in magazine and newspaper columns) is not the same thing as a true, meaningful, in-depth understanding of astrology but is clearly used "for entertainment purposes" only. No wonder those columns are usually placed on the same page as the comics and crossword puzzle. All too often, it seems evident that anyone who initially attempts to debunk astrology yet actually spends some time endeavoring to learn more details about the subject will eventually become a proponent and practitioner instead.

According to astrologer Steven Forrest, there exists a "fear" of astrology among its more modern critics, which he labels as "astrophobia":

> My premise, in a nutshell, is this: there exists a pervasive perceptual bias among those "normal," "rational" people who feel emotionally compelled to criticize astrology. The bias functions on an unconscious level, driving them towards otherwise inexplicable behaviors characterized by denial, anger, inappropriate assumption of authority, and illogic. The trigger for these behaviors is broad, broader by far than astrology. In fact, it embraces approximately half of the total spectrum of experience available to human consciousness. The triggering stimulus is the suggestion that rational processes might—in any way—be influenced by irrational or "transrational" processes (Forrest 1993, 36).

In Forrest's argument, the dichotomy between the two spectrums of human experience pertains to the two sides or the hemispheric influence of the brain. The right hemisphere of the brain is commonly linked with intuition, and the left hemisphere of the brain is commonly linked with logic. While the scientific discovery of the hemispheric influence in the brain obviously occurred fairly recently, a certain duality has always existed between the opposing realms of intuition and logic.

By insisting upon only a logical explanation for an otherwise irrational or nonlogical phenomenon, the detractors of astrology, or of any mystical subject for that matter, deny a place for intuition and right-brain intelligence. Clearly, the experiences of religion, spiritual belief, or any type of spiritual awakening are included in the long list of nonlogical phenomena. Apparently then, by denying a right-sided intelligence, these detractors insist we use only one-half of the total power of our brains.

Nevertheless, many great thinkers in mathematics and science were astrologers; those names include Galileo, Copernicus, Johannes Kepler, Leonardo Da Vinci, Benjamin Franklin, and Carl Jung. Even US President Ronald Reagan used an astrologer's services (through his wife, Nancy Reagan) when he was president. During his presidency, there was never any overt criticism of his astrological practice published in the press.

Therefore, do not be frightened when astrology is attacked by the misinformed. Above all, keep an open mind and remember that a minister or preacher is only human and is capable of making a mistake. Pray for him or her to learn the truth along with others.

There are many good books on the market introducing astrology, and many good websites on various topics in astrology. Some of these resources are listed in the appendix. When learning astrology, remember you are learning an ancient and symbolic language, a system of looking at the world with its own unique perspective. Like any topic worth learning in depth, it requires a great deal of time, effort, and commitment. Just take it a little bit at a time.

And we should always remember what Jesus Christ told us in the book of Revelation, even on the very last page of the Bible, when he said:

> *I Jesus have sent mine angel to testify unto you these things in the churches. I am the root and offspring of David, and the bright and morning star* (Revelation 22:16).

As the bright and morning star, Jesus perfectly illuminates the profound beauty and goodness of God's celestial creation. And thus, for all of us who have the desire to see, you can find the sign of Jesus every morning that you care to look. You need only to look up.

LIST OF CHARTS

Justification: The date and time for charts 1 and 2 were selected according to the close correspondence between the chart's Great Conjunction and other documented historical evidence surrounding King David's life.

Justification: Charts 3 and 4 portray the exact time of the solar eclipse occurring in Bethlehem in March of 5 BCE. The charts are pertinent to documented historical evidence surrounding the birth, life, and crucifixion of Jesus Christ.

All charts utilize software purchased from Solar Fire Gold

LIST OF ASTROLOGICAL SYMBOLS

THE ZODIAC SIGNS AND PLANETS

Signs		Planets	
♈ Aries	♎ Libra	☉ Sun	♃ Jupiter
♉ Taurus	♏ Scorpio	☽ Moon	♄ Saturn
♊ Gemini	♐ Sagittarius	☿ Mercury	♅ Uranus
♋ Cancer	♑ Capricorn	♀ Venus	♆ Neptune
♌ Leo	♒ Aquarius	♂ Mars	♇ Pluto
♍ Virgo	♓ Pisces		

THE MAJOR ASPECTS IN ASTROLOGY

Name	Symbol	Degrees	Signs (usually)
CONJUNCTION	☌	0º	Same sign
OPPOSITION	☍	180º	6 signs
SQUARE	☐	90º	3 signs
TRINE	△	120º	4 signs
SEXTILE	✳	60º	2 signs

BIBLIOGRAPHY AND REFERENCES

Alchin, Linda. "Causes for the Fall of the Roman Empire." n.d.a. www.tribunesandtriumphs.org/roman-empire/causes-for-the-fall-of-the-roman-empire.htm, accessed February 2015.

———. "Reason Why the Roman Empire Fell." n.d.b. www.tribunesandtriumphs.org/roman-empire/reason-why-the-roman-empire-fell.htm, accessed February 2015.

Andrews, Evan. "8 Reasons Why Rome Fell." January 14, 2014. www.history.com/news/history-lists/8-reasons-why-rome-fell, accessed February 2015.

Arroyo, Steven. *Astrology, Karma & Transformation: The Inner Dimensions of the Birth Chart.* 2nd ed. Sebastopol, CA: CRCS Publications, 1992.

Astrology News Service. http://astrologynewsservice.com.

Augustinus, Aurelius. *The Confessions of St. Augustine.* Translated by Edward B. Pusey. New York: P. F. Collier & Son, 1909a.

———. *The Imitation of Christ.* Translated by Thomas A. Kempis. New York: P. F. Collier & Son, 1909b.

———. *The City of God.* Translated by Marcus Dods. New York: Modern Library, Random House, 1950.

Bible Study Organization. www.bible.study.org/bibleref/meaning-of-numbers-in-bible/7.html.

Biblical Training. "Host of Heaven." n.d. www.biblicaltraining.org/library/host-heaven, accessed August 2016.

Bock, Darrell, PhD, Research Professor, Dallas Theological Seminary. See www.dts.edu/faculty for educational background and biographical information. Cited by Joe Sooner at www.religiousmusings.blogspot.com/2006/11/mary-Magdalene_13.html, accessed February 2017.

Cameron, Averil. "The Reign of Constantine, A.D. 306–307." In *The Cambridge Ancient History.* Vol. 12, *The Crisis of Empire, A.D. 193–337.* Edited by Alan K. Bowman, Averil Cameron, and Peter Garnsey, 90–109. Cambridge, UK: Cambridge University Press, 2005.

Campion, Nicholas. *A History of Western Astrology.* Vol. 1, *The Ancient and Classical Worlds.* London: Bloomsbury Academic, 2008.

———. *Astrology and Cosmology in the World's Religions.* New York and London: New York University Press, 2012.

Carr, David, and Coleen M. Conway. *An Introduction to the Bible: Sacred Texts and Imperial Contexts.* West Sussex, UK: Wiley-Blackwell, 2010.

Carter, Charles E. O. *Essays on the Foundations of Astrology.* London: Theosophical Publishing House, 1978.

Catholic Online News Consortium. "Here Are 10 Very Interesting Facts about the Catholic Church You Probably Didn't Know!" November 18, 2014. www.Catholic.org/news/hf/faith/story.php?id=57689, accessed October 2016.

Chadwick, Henry. "The Early Christian Community." In *The Oxford Illustrated History of Christianity.* Edited by John McManners, 21–61. Oxford: Oxford University Press, 1990.

Clifford, Frank. "75 Critical Degrees." n.d. www.astrologyuniversity.com/study-materials/article/75-critical-degrees, accessed January 2017.

Coffman, Elesha. "What Is the Origin of the Christian Fish Symbol?" August 2008. www.christianitytoday.com/history/2008/august/what-is-origin-of-christian-fish-symbol.html, accessed March 2015.

Coogan, Michael D., and W. Sibley Towner. "Daniel." In *The Oxford Guide to People & Places of the Bible.* Edited by Bruce M. Metzer and Michael D. Coogan, 48–50. New York: Oxford University Press, 2001.

Detweiler, Nancy B., M.Div. "History of Astrology in Judaism & Christianity." March 5, 2012. *The Way of Love Blog.* https://pathwaytoascension.wordpress.com/2012/03/05/history-of-astrology-in-judaism-christianity, accessed October 2016.

Dixon, Jeane. *Yesterday, Today, and Forever: How Astrology Can Help You Find Your Place in God's Plan.* Kansas City, MO: Andrews, McMeel & Parker, 1987.

Doane, Doris Chase. *Horoscopes Reveal Personalities.* Tempe, AZ: American Federation of Astrologers, 1995.

Dobin, Joel C. "To Rule Both Day and Night: Astrology in the Bible, Midrash & Talmud." 2012. Quoted online by Nancy B. Detweiler, M.Div., at https://pathwaytoascension.wordpress.com/2012/03/05/history-of-astrology-in-judaism-christanity, accessed October 2016.

Encyclopedia Britannica. "The City of God." n.d. *Encyclopedia Britannica.* www.britannica.com/topic/The-City-of-God, accessed February 2017.

Everything Heaven. www.EverythingHeaven.com, accessed October 2016.

Eysenck, Hans J., and David Nias. *Astrology: Science or Superstition?* London: Penguin, 1982.

Forrest, Steven. *The Night Speaks: A Meditation on the Astrological Worldview.* San Diego, CA: ACS Publications, 1993.

Fosdick, Harry Emerson, ed. *Great Voices of the Reformation: An Anthology.* New York: Modern Library, Random House, 1952.

Franklin, Benjamin. *Poor Richard's Almanack,* 1732 to 1758.

Funk & Wagnalls. *Standard Desk Dictionary.* 2 vols. New York: Harper & Row, 1984.

Galli, Mike. "Mary Magdalene (1st Century A.D.)." 2005, rev. 2018. http://departments.kings.edu/womens_history/marymagda.html/, accessed February 2017.

George, Demetra. *Astrology and the Authentic Self: Integrating Traditional and Modern Astrology to Uncover the Essence of the Birth Chart.* Lake Worth, FL: Ibis, 2008.

Gill, N. S. "The Star of Bethlehem and Dating of the Birth of Jesus." March 8, 2017. www.ancienthistory.about.com/od/churchhistory/qt/121507/JesusBirth.htm, accessed December 2014.

Grant, Ernest A., and Catherine T. Grant. Grant Textbook Series. 4 vols. 2nd ed. Tempe, AZ: American Federation of Astrologers, 2008–2010.

Gunn, David M. "David." In *The Oxford Guide to People & Places of the Bible.* Edited by Bruce M. Metzer and Michael D. Coogan, 51–54. New York: Oxford University Press, 2001.

Hale, John R., PhD, Professor, University of Louisville. Lecturer in *Exploring the Roots of Religion—Part 3, Lecture 33: Taking Religions Underground at Rome.* Chantilly, VA: Great Courses from the Teaching Company, 2009.

Harl, Kenneth W., PhD, Professor, Tulane University. Lecturer in *Great Ancient Civilizations of Asia Minor—Part 2, Lecture 14: Rome versus the Kings of the East.* Chantilly, VA: Great Courses from the Teaching Company, 2001a.

———. Lecturer in *Great Ancient Civilizations of Asia Minor—Part 2, Lecture 15: Prosperity and Roman Patronage.* Chantilly, VA: Great Courses from the Teaching Company, 2001b.

———. Lecturer in *Great Ancient Civilizations of Asia Minor—Part 2, Lecture 17: Jews and Early Christians.* Chantilly, VA: Great Courses from the Teaching Company, 2001c.

———. Lecturer in *Great Ancient Civilizations of Asia Minor—Part 2, Lecture 18: From Rome to Byzantium.* Chantilly, VA: Great Courses from the Teaching Company, 2001d.

Harrelson, Walter. *Interpreting the Old Testament.* New York: Holt, Rinehart, and Winston, 1964.

Haskins, Susan. *Mary Magdalen: Myth and Metaphor.* New York: Riverhead Books, 1993.

———. Stated in the documentary film *Secrets of the Code,* produced by Donald Zuckerman, Dan Burstein, and Brian Edelman. Mexico City: Alchemist Films, 2006. Available for purchase at www.SonyPictures.com.

Hawkins, Gerald S., in collaboration with John B. White. *Stonehenge Decoded.* Garden City, NY: Doubleday, 1965.

Hegedus, Tim. *Early Christianity and Ancient Astrology.* New York: Peter Lang, 2007.

Holden, James Herschel. *A History of Horoscopic Astrology.* Tempe, AZ: American Federation of Astrologers, 2006.

Holy Bible, Authorized King James Version. Iowa Falls, IA: World Bible Publishers, 1994.

Holy Bible, the New King James Version. Nashville, TN: Thomas Nelson, 1982.

Houghton, S. M. *Sketches from Church History.* Edinburgh: Banner of Truth Trust, 1995.

Humphreys, Colin. "The Star of Bethlehem." *Science and Christian Belief* 5 (October 1994): 83–101. www.asa3.org/ASA/topicsAstronomy-Cosmology/S&CB%2010-93Humphreys.html, accessed December 2014.

Ibn Ezra, Avraham Ben Meir. *The Beginning of Wisdom.* Translated by Meira B. Epstein. Archive for the Retrieval of Historical Astrological Texts (ARHAC), 1998.

Jacobi, Max. "Astrology." In *The Catholic Encyclopedia.* Vol. 2. Edited by Charles G. Herbermann, Edward

A. Pace, Condé B. Pallen, Thomas J. Shahan, and John J. Wynne, 18–25. New York: Robert Appleton, 1907. www.ncwadvent.org/cathen/02018e.html, accessed February 2017.

Jacobus, Helen R. "The Zodiac Sign Names in the Dead Sea Scrolls (4Q318): Features and Questions." PhD diss., University of Manchester, 2009. http://academia.edu/5986690/The_Zodiac_Sign_Names_in_the_Dead_Sea_Scrolls_4Q318_Features_and_Questions.

Josephus, Flavius. "The Antiquities of the Jews, Book 1: Concerning the Interval of Three Thousand Eight Hundred and Thirty-Three Years; From the Creation to the Death of Isaac." In The Complete Works of Flavius Josephus. Translated by William Whiston, 1737. London: Forgotten Books, 2015. Quotation found in chap. 2:3. Other pertinent sections concerning Abraham and astrology include chaps. 7:1 and 8:2. www.ultimatebiblereferencelibrary.com/Complete_Works_of _Josephus.pdf.

Kelly, J. N. D. Early Christian Creeds. New York: David McKay, 1972.

Kent, Charles Foster. History of the Hebrew People: From the Settlement in Canaan to the Division of the Kingdom. New York: Charles Scribner's Sons, 1908.

Kochunas, Brad. Communication published in International Society for Astrological Research E-zine 885 (March 13, 2016).

Lehman, J. Lee. Classical Astrology for Modern Living: From Ptolemy to Psychology & Back Again. Atglen, PA: Whitford Press, a division of Schiffer, 1996.

———. Astrology of Sustainability. Atglen, PA: Schiffer, 2011.

Lilly, William. Christian Astrology. First published in 1647. Bel Air, MD: Astrology Classics, 2004.

Luther, Martin. "Concerning Christian Liberty." In Great Voices of the Reformation: An Anthology. Edited by Harry Emerson Fosdick, 81–95. New York: Modern Library, Random House, 1952a.

———. "Luther's Reply at the Diet of Worms." In Great Voices of the Reformation: An Anthology. Edited by Harry Emerson Fosdick, 76–80. New York: Modern Library, Random House, 1952b.

Manchester, William. A World Lit Only by Fire: The Medieval Mind and the Renaissance; Portrait of an Age. Boston: Little, Brown, 1992.

Marcarelli, Joyce. Faith Unconquered: The Roman Persecution of Early Christians. DVD. Executive produced by Charles R. Weber. Reader's Digest Ancient Worlds Brought to Life. Chicago: Questar Video, 1991.

March, Marion D., and Joan McEvers. The Only Way to Learn Astrology. Vol. 1, Basic Principles. 2nd ed. Exeter, NH: ACS Publications, 2008.

———. The Only Way to Learn Astrology. Vol. 2, Math & Interpretation Techniques. 2nd ed. San Diego, CA: ACS Publications, 2009.

Marcus, Robert. "From Rome to the Barbarian Kingdoms (330–700)." In The Oxford Illustrated History of Christianity. Edited by John McManners, 62–91. Oxford: Oxford University Press, 1990.

Matthews, Caitlin, codirector of the Institute for Mystical Studies. Stated in the documentary film Secrets of the Code, produced by Donald Zuckerman, Dan Burstein, and Brian Edelman. Mexico City: Alchemist Films, 2006. Available for purchase at www.SonyPictures.com.

McDonald, Gary J. "Why Christianity Rejected Reincarnation." Wisdom Magazine, February 2011. www.wisdom-magazine.com/Article.aspx/2043/, accessed October 2016.

Mitchell, John. Megalithomania: Artists, Antiquarians, and Archaeologists at the Old Stone Monuments. Ithaca, NY: Cornell University Press, 1982.

Morris, Henry M. The New Defender's Study Bible. Nashville, TN: World Publishing, 2006. Cited by the Institute for Creation Research at www.icr.org/bible/genesis/1:14, accessed December 2015.

New World Encyclopedia. "Star of David." In New World Encyclopedia. October 21, 2015. http://newworldencyclopedia.org/p/index.php?title=/Star_of_David&oldid=991455, accessed February 2017.

Newton, Isaac. Cited in "Keynes MS.28." In The Chymistry of Isaac Newton. Edited by William R. Newman. Bloomington: Indiana University, 2010. www.dlib.indiana.edu/newton/mss/dipl/ALCH00017, accessed February 2017.

Noble, Thomas F. X., PhD, Professor, University of Notre Dame. Lecturer in The Foundations of Western Civilization—Part 1, Lecture 4: The Hebrews; Small States and Big Ideas. Chantilly, VA: Great Courses from the Teaching Company, 2002a.

———. Lecturer in The Foundations of Western Civilization—Part 3, Lecture 31: Barbarian Kingdoms in the West. Chantilly, VA: Great Courses from the Teaching Company, 2002b.

———. Lecturer in The Foundations of Western Civilization—Part 3, Lecture 35: The Chivalrous Society. Chantilly, VA: Great Courses from the Teaching Company, 2002c.

Pagels, Elaine, PhD, Professor of Religion, Princeton University. Stated in the documentary film Secrets of the Code, produced by Donald Zuckerman, Dan Burstein, and Brian Edelman. Mexico City: Alchemist Films, 2006. Available for purchase at www.SonyPictures.com.

Papini, Giovanni. "Life of Christ." Translated by Dorothy Canfield Fisher. In Reader's Digest Family Treasury of Great Biographies. Pleasantville, NY: Reader's Digest Association, 1970.

Perry, Glenn, PhD. Communication published in *International Society for Astrological Research E-zine* 914 (October 2, 2016).

———. AstroPsychology Services. www.aaperry.com.

Popovic, Mladen. *Reading the Human Body: Physionomics and Astrology in the Dead Sea Scrolls and Hellenistic—Early Roman Period Judaism.* Leiden, The Netherlands: Brill, 2007.

Portalié, Eugène. "Saint Augustine of Hippo." In *The Catholic Encyclopedia.* Vol. 2. Edited by Charles G. Herbermann, Edward A. Pace, Condé B. Pallen, Thomas J. Shahan, and John J. Wynne, 84–104. New York: Robert Appleton, 1907. www.newadvent.org/cathen/02084a.htm, accessed February 2017.

Pyle, Jack, and Taylor Reese. *Raising with the Moon: The Complete Guide to Gardening and Living by the Signs of the Moon.* Boone, NC: Parkway, 1993.

Rambo, Tye. "Tertullian on Baptism." March 2010. www.biblicalspirituality.fies.wordpress.com/2010/03/Tertullian-on-baptism-by-tye-rambo.pdf, accessed February 2017.

Rudhyar, Dane. *The Astrology of Personality: A Reformulation of Astrological Concepts and Ideals, in Terms of Contemporary Psychology and Philosophy.* Garden City, NY: Doubleday, 1970.

Schnürer, Gustav. "States of the Church." In *The Catholic Encyclopedia.* Vol. 14. Edited by Charles G. Herbermann, Edward A. Pace, Condé B. Pallen, Thomas J. Shahan, and John J. Wynne, 257–268. New York: Robert Appleton, 1912. www.newadvent.org/cathen/14257a.htm, accessed February 2017.

Shakespeare, William. *Julius Caesar*, act 1, scene 2. www.shakespeare-navigators.com/JC_Navigator/JC_1_2.html, accessed February 2015.

Showalter, Daniel N. "Magi." In *The Oxford Guide to People & Places of the Bible.* Edited by Bruce M. Metzer and Michael D. Coogan, 187–188. New York: Oxford University Press, 2001.

Sooner, Joe. "Mary Magdalene. 2006. www.religiousmusings.blogspot.com/2006/11/mary-Magdalene_13.html, accessed September 2016.

Tabor, James D. *The Jesus Dynasty: The Hidden History of Jesus, His Royal Family, and the Birth of Christianity.* New York: Simon & Schuster, 2006.

Tarnas, Richard. *Cosmos and Psyche: Intimations of a New World View.* New York: Plume, 2007.

Thomas, Robert B. *The Old Farmer's Almanac 2000.* Dublin, NH: Yankee, 1999.

Tompkins, Sue. *The Contemporary Astrologer's Handbook: An In-Depth Guide to Interpreting Your Horoscope.* London: Flare in conjunction with the London School of Astrology, 2006.

Tyl, Noel. *Synthesis and Counseling in Astrology: The Professional Manual.* Woodbury, MN: Llewelyn, 2009.

United with Israel. "The Menorah: Seven Branches or Nine?" 2015. www.unitedwithisrael.org/the-menorah-vs-the-chanukiah, accessed January 2015.

van der Meer, Fredric. *Augustine the Bishop: The Life and Work of a Father of the Church.* Translated by Brian Battershaw and G. R. Lamb. New York: Sheed and Ward, 1961.

Weiss, Brian L. *Many Lives, Many Masters.* New York: Simon & Schuster, 1988.

Wellman, Jack. "What Does the Number Seven (7) Mean or Represent in the Bible?" 2014a. www.patheos.com/blogs/christiancrier/2014/09/26/what-does-the-number-seven-7-mean-or-represent-in-the-bible, accessed March 2016.

———. "What Does the Number Twelve (12) Mean or Represent in the Bible?" 2014b. www.patheos.com/blogs/christiancrier/2014/09/28/what-does-the-number-twelve-12-mean-or-represent-in-the-bible, accessed March 2016.

Zain, C. C. Quoted on p. 95 by Doris Chase Doane in *Horoscopes Reveal Personalities.* Tempe, AZ: American Federation of Astrologers, 1995.

Zappala, Aldo, dir. *Great Cities of the Ancient World: Rome and Pompei.* Executive produced by Albert J. Nader. *Reader's Digest* Ancient Worlds Brought to Life. Chicago: Questar Video, 1994.

SUGGESTED READING FOR FURTHER STUDY

Helpful Websites Developed by Astrology Professionals

American Federation of Astrologers, Inc. (AFA). www.astrologers.com.

Provides networking opportunities, sells books for all levels of astrology, and gives information on conventions and events. Offers a specially selected beginner's learning package.

AstroDatabank. www.astro.com/astro-databank/Main_Page.

A free read-only database, useful for finding reliable birth information for notable or famous people.

Astrodienst. www.astro.com.

Provides a free tool to draw individual horoscopes by entering personal birth data; offers additional astrology services for sale.

Astrology News Service. www.astrologynewsservice.com.

Free articles on newsworthy items related to astrology, including interviews, book reviews, and information on conferences.

International Society for Astrological Research (ISAR). www.isarastrology.org.

Supports astrological research, provides community and networking opportunities, sets ethical and professional standards, and offers various symposium recordings and training opportunities.

National Council for Geocosmic Research. www.geocosmic.org.

Provides information on networking opportunities, classes, meetings, and conferences.

Mountain Astrologer Magazine. http://mountainastrologer.com.

Sells subscriptions to a bimonthly magazine devoted to astrological topics; many articles are written by highly rated astrologers; provides a student section in every issue.

Selected Titles for Beginners of Astrology

Carter, Charles E. O. *Essays on the Foundations of Astrology*. London: Theosophical Publishing House, 1978.

Grant, Ernest A., and Catherine T. Grant. *Grant Textbook Series*. 4 vols. Tempe, AZ: American Federation of Astrologers, 1988.

March, Marion D., and Joan McEvers. *The Only Way to Learn Astrology Series*. 4 vols. 2nd ed. Exeter, NH, and San Diego, CA: ASC Publications, 1999–2010.

Tompkins, Sue. *The Contemporary Astrologer's Handbook: An In–Depth Guide to Interpreting Your Horoscope*. London: Flare in conjunction with the London School of Astrology, 2006.

Selected Titles in the Philosophy of Astrology

Arroyo, Stephen. *Astrology, Karma, and Transformation: The Inner Dimensions of the Birth Chart*. 2nd ed. Sebastopol, CA: CRCS Publications, 1992.

Rudhyar, Dane. *The Astrology of Personality: A Re-formulation of Astrological Concepts and Ideals, in Terms of Contemporary Psychology and Philosophy*. Garden City, NY: Doubleday, 1970.

Tarnas, Richard. *Cosmos and Psyche: Intimations of a New World View*. New York: Plume, 2007.

Selected Titles in the History of Astrology

Campion, Nicholas. *A History of Western Astrology*. Vol. 1, *The Ancient and Classical Worlds*. London: Bloomsbury Academic, 2008.

———. *Astrology and Cosmology in the World's Religions*. New York and London: New York University Press, 2012.

Hegedus, Tim. *Early Christianity and Ancient Astrology*. New York: Peter Lang, 2007.

Holden, James. *A History of Horoscopic Astrology*. Tempe, AZ: American Federation of Astrologers, 2006.

SUZAN STEPHAN

Suzan Stephan became a Christian at a young age and has studied astrology almost her entire life. Finding the understanding of astrology to be spiritually significant, Suzan felt compelled to explain and legitimatize astrology for the benefit of all Christians. Suzan sincerely believes that a core understanding of the astrological birth chart is the perfect means for understanding God's plan for the individual.